"Our"

U.S. National Debt

101

= = =

A Shameful Liberty-Threatening Legacy
Being Passed To America's Young Children,
Grandchildren, & The Not Yet Born

William James Moore

"Knowledge will forever govern ignorance, and a people who mean to be their own Governors, must arm themselves with the power knowledge gives." — James Madison (1751 – 1836)

"To sit back hoping that someday, someway, someone will make things right is to go on feeding the crocodile, hoping he will eat you last — but eat you he will." — Ronald Reagan (1911-2004)

"It does not require a majority to prevail, but rather an irate, tireless minority keen to set brush fires in people's minds." — Samuel Adams (1722-1803)

"All that is necessary for the triumph of evil is for good men [and women] to do nothing." — Edmund Burke (1729-1797)

"Our lives begin to end the day we become silent about things that matter." — Plato (428/427 or 424/423BC – 348/347 BC)

= = =

Dedication

To our grandson Matthew "Matt"

May Matthew and other U.S. citizen recipients of our nation's many priceless opportunities, demanding responsibilities, and awesome challenges, be blessed with the means, desire, and commitment to experience, enjoy, respect, protect, and pass on to future generations, an America of inalienable (God-given) Rights to life, liberty, and pursuit of happiness.

"In the beginning God created the heaven and the earth."
— Genesis 1:1

Contents

In Remembrance of
Our Mothers and Fathers

To my mother, Hazel; Ann's mother, Lillie; my natural father, James; Ann's natural father, Robert; Ann's stepfather, George; and my stepfathers Ernest and Marvin. Each, a once young child with curiosity, awe, plans, and dreams. Born into daunting economic circumstances of the Great Depression (the deepest, longest-lasting, and most wide-spread economic depression of the 20th Century)—involving severe economic circumstances far beyond any true understanding of we later generations. Like so many others of that time, each, along with their families, often faced with life-consuming focus on basic survival. Challenged by limited education and scarce, often extremely- hazardous and physically-demanding work environments. A world where attitudes of being "owed, deserving, entitled, and a victim" had no welcome or relevance. With the "how to" as spouses, parents, and grandparents, derived from learn-as-you-go and the school of often harsh challenges. Their respective strengths, weaknesses, failures, and successes, not always equally recognized, understood, shared, or otherwise experienced within family. Each an enviable example of giving and self-sacrifice. Loving parents who did and gave their best. Leaving a legacy of vital life-lessons, treasured experiences, and cherished memories. So deeply and dearly loved by so many—and now longed for and missed beyond words. ♥

Special Appreciation

To my wife Ann; daughter Jamie; son Ryan, grandson Matthew, and Mike H. And to other "Family"—all with whom we have been, and may yet be, privileged to share treasured relationships and priceless memories.

= = =

"A family is a bunch of people who keep confusing you with someone you were as a kid." — Robert Brault

"I know why families were created with all their imperfections. They humanize you. They are made to make you forget yourself occasionally, so that the beautiful balance of life is not destroyed."
— Anais Nin

"Children begin by loving their parents; as they grow older they judge them; sometimes they forgive them." -Oscar Wilde

"We all have our strengths and our failings. — Hannah Simone

"Enjoy the little things, for one day you may look back and realize they were the big things." — Robert Brault

"Sometimes you will never know the value of a moment until it becomes a memory." — Dr. Seuss

"Other things may change us, but we start and end with family."
— Anthony Brandt

Recognition

It is most doubtful that any book has ever been written "totally alone." Certainly, this one was not. For, in supplement to my personal life experiences, observations, and views, the content of this writing was drawn from that of countless known and unknown others. All to whom I express sincere appreciation for the enlightenment shared and access to crucial information.

= = =

"As we express our gratitude, we must never forget that the highest appreciation is not to utter words, but to live by them."
– John F. Kennedy (1917-1963)

"Those who expect to reap the blessings of freedom, must, like men, undergo the fatigue of supporting it." —Thomas Paine (1737-1809)

"Government exists to protect us from each other. Where government has gone beyond its limits is in deciding to protect us from ourselves." – Ronald Reagan (1911-2004)

"The welfare of our country is the great object to which our cares and efforts ought to be directed." – George Washington, 01/09/1790

Introduction

> *"America will never be destroyed from the outside. If we falter and lose our freedoms, it will be because we destroyed ourselves.* —Abraham Lincoln (1809–1865), 16th U.S. President
>
> *"I am not arrogant enough to tell you what the future holds, but I am faithful enough to remind you who holds the future."*
> — Steve Maraboli (1975-)

Dear Reader,

There are countless examples of "good," "greatness," and "things done proper" throughout our Nation and the World. Those positive and uplifting sides of humankind. None the least the unique and much sought after nature of liberty and opportunity thus far available only in America. However, and importantly so, this writing is not about such things.

Rather, this book is about a human-created "menace." One posing a rapidly increasing threat to the future of our country's children and grandchildren of today and generations not yet born. A menace to their liberty and livelihood, in large measure the result of, and continuing to feed upon, wide-spread ignorance, apathy, complacency, denial, and greed. More specifically, this writing is about our rapidly growing and very much out of control U.S. National Debt!

Given today's technology, few if any of us can rightfully claim ignorance or otherwise unawareness of this rapidly growing peril. For example, wide spread access to the Internet has made readily available an overwhelming array of information sources on this subject. Including, but not limited to, untold numbers of books, charts, graphs, studies, reports, news articles, websites, YouTube videos, etc. Even a **U.S. National Debt Clock: Real Time"** (physically installed and publically displayed in New York City since 1989; presently located at One Bryant Park, west of Sixth Avenue between 42nd and 43rd Streets in New York; and for years Internet-accessible at **http://www.usdebtclock.org/**).

Therefore, with this subject long covered by an overwhelming number of already available information sources—why then, this another book? The answer, at least from this writer's view, has much to do with a mix of concern, guilt, frustration, and personal need.

More specifically, **concern** about the ultimate consequences of our unsustainable National Debt; **guilt** for being in any fashion a contributor to such a menace, and for passing such on to our children, grandchildren, and future generations of Americans; **frustration** about how such a threat can continue to be treated with such gross unconcern and suicidal inattention by so many of us; and a **personal need** that seems best explained by Helen Keller's quotation at the close of this *Introduction*.

In undertaking this writing it was, and remains, respectfully recognized that many highly complicated and politically sensitive issues are involved in "why" our U.S. National Debt exists and "how" to fix it. Issues debated by our country's most capable economists, politicians, business leaders, and others. Nevertheless, it was likewise considered that these same "complexities and sensitivities" may very likely be among the major reasons our nation's debt crisis is often "tuned out" by so many. And with that prospect in mind, a serious effort has been made to help this book's message avoid the same fate. Through the use of generalized content intentionally limited in terms of range of topics, depth of detail, and overall volume (number of pages).

As a result, hopefully this particular material will "at least delay" the natural human instinct to "avoid the unpleasant." At least long enough to gain a constructive grasp of the inescapable certainty that a time of reckoning will one day arrive. The time when "kicking-the-can" of responsibility down the road, and further borrowing from "Peter to pay Paul," are no longer options. When the foreign and domestic holders of our National Debt will expect and demand payment. When promises made are expected to be honored.

And, may our focus on this material also be long enough to grasp and accept that irresponsible government spending, and our resulting out-of-control National Debt, are the outcome of our "choices" — some made through ignorance; some with shameful intent. As are policies that continue to dump the awesome burden of such debt on the backs of future generations of Americans.

Therefore, it is sincerely hoped that something within these pages (and/or gained elsewhere) serves to meaningfully encourage and support our undeniable duty to make more responsible choices. Choices that lead us to strive in our own respectively capable ways, as individuals, groups, and through our elected government representatives, to bring our National Debt crisis under timely and responsible control.

While never forgetting that the critical threat posed by our unsustainable U.S. National Debt is very much "real." As will also be the legacy one day left by us — our country's now in-charge adults in the room. History will long note that we either met our responsibility, or shamefully chose to pass on to others the unwarranted and unthinkable burdens and suffering of unmanageable debt from irresponsible spending. Our duty to one another and future generations of Americans is inescapably clear. Remaining much uncertain, however — is if, when, and how, we ultimately choose to measure up.

= = =

"I am only one, but still I am one. I cannot do everything, but still I can do something; and because I cannot do everything, I will not refuse to do something that I can do." — *Helen Keller (1880-1968), American author, political activist and lecturer, and first deafblind person to earn a Bachelor of Arts degree.*

"Our"
U.S. National Debt –
In Brief

> *"I place economy among the first and most important virtues, and public debt as the greatest of dangers to be feared...To preserve our independence, we must not let our rulers load us with perpetual debt...We must make our choice between economy and liberty or profusion and servitude..."* *– Thomas Jefferson (1743–1826)*

Commonly defined, our U.S. National Debt is the total of all outstanding debt owed by the federal government. And since in our constitutional republic "we" U.S. citizens are ultimately "the government," the National Debt is likewise "ours."

Historically speaking, a National Debt has been a part of our country since its beginning. The earliest record of such was prepared by Alexander Hamilton, the first U.S. Treasury Secretary and self-taught economist. Following the Revolutionary War, his 1790 analysis showed our National Debt to be about $75 million. A debt thereafter fueled over the centuries by additional wars, and by other circumstances driving government spending well beyond the funds it takes in. Fast-forwarding about 216 years later to 1906, the year my dad was born, our National Debt was a little more than $2 billion. When my wife and I entered the world it had increased to $201 billion. Around arrival of our two children it was about $427 billion, and by 1981 had reached $1 trillion. By 2003, the year we were blessed with our (the World's best-ever) grandson, it had jumped to $6.7 trillion, and by 2008 had climbed to more than $10 trillion. **And by 2018, the year of this writing, had exceeded $21 trillion!**

Our **U.S. National Debt** is managed by the U.S. Treasury Department through its Bureau of the Public Debt, and made up of the combination of the following two broad categories:

(1.) **Public Deb**t: This is money our federal government borrows from American investors; foreign investors; foreign governments; etc., through the sale of U.S. Treasury Bills, Notes, and Bonds; U.S. Savings Bonds; etc. *In 2018, this Public Debt portion amounted to about $15.8 trillion (about 75 percent of the total National Debt).*

(2.) *Intra-governmental Debt:* This is money our federal government owes itself. Such as money borrowed from the Social Security and Medicare trust funds; Military Retirement funds; Civil Service funds; Federal Reserve Banks; etc. *In 2018, this Intra-governmental Debt portion amounted to about $5.2 trillion (about 25 percent of the total National Debt).*

In total, this **$21 trillion National Debt** amounts to about:

- $64,562 for every U.S. citizen, or
- $174,190 for every U.S. taxpayer, or
- 5 times yearly federal government tax revenues

Furthermore, **$21 trillion** also "exceeded" our nation's 2017 Gross Domestic Product (GDP), i.e., the total value of all goods and services produced in the U.S. for the year. And, as shown in the Chart below, the last time our National Debt was "more than" our GDP was during the 1945–1947 time frame, when paying for World War II.

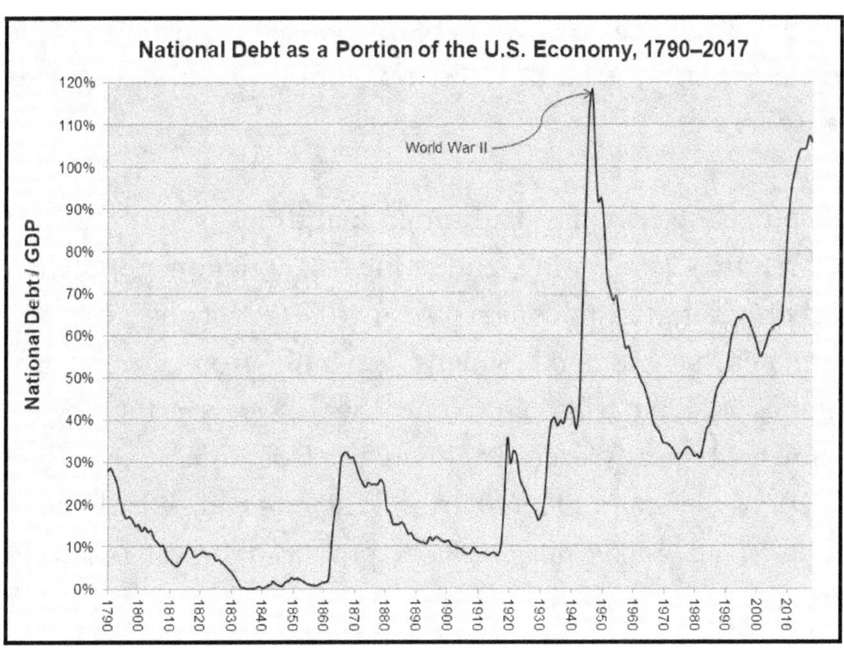

<u>Unfunded Liabilities – "The Elephant in the room"</u>: As staggering as the so far noted **$21 trillion** debt figure truly is, it makes up only part of our federal government's total debt obligation. That is, only the portion that is **legally binding**. It doesn't include other portions, such as the federal government's **Unfunded Liabilities**.

An **Unfunded Liability** is basically the amount, at any given time, by which future payment obligations exceed the present and forecasted value of the funds available to pay those obligations. In other words, the amount of money the government has "promised" to people, but in all likelihood will not be able to pay and is also not legally required to pay. **For example, the unsustainable promises regarding future Social Security, Medicare, Federal Employee, and Veterans benefits, etc**.

Of course, determining **Unfunded Liabilities** is very difficult and requires "estimating" future interest, inflation, population growth, mortality rates, etc. As a result, over the years the estimates have ranged widely; generally from around $80 trillion to $200 trillion. None the less, even the lowest estimates typically exceed the yearly gross domestic product (GDP) of the entire planet Earth. Which of course is the total value of all goods and services produced by all countries worldwide during a given year.

For example, the global GDP for 2018 has been projected to be about $84.4 trillion. Whereas, our **U.S. Federal Government's**

"Unfunded Liabilities" for 2018 have been estimated to exceed **$112 trillion**. Amounting to more than:

- **$344,666** for every U.S. citizen, or
- **$930,115** for every U.S. taxpayer.

It is also disturbingly noteworthy, that the biggest share of the above referenced **Unfunded Liabilities** consist of not backed up promises to future recipients of Social Security, Medicare and Veterans benefits.

Truly our federal government's **Unfunded Liabilities** are the **"elephant in the room"** no one wants to talk about! Least of all, those among us who continue to demand more and more so-called "free stuff." And the politicians who are willing to feed such out-of-control greed with unsustainable promises financed by more and more debt. Debt that "we the people" are ultimately accountable for.

But wait! There is more! Our $21 trillion National Debt number also does not include certain so-called "Agency Debt." That is, the amount of outstanding debt issued by various Federal Agencies, such as, the Federal Home Loan Bank (FHLB) and the "Ginnie Mae" – Government National Mortgage Association (GNMA), as well as government-sponsored enterprises, such as Fannie Mae and Freddie Mac.

Historically, Agency Debt has not been included in the total U.S. National Debt as published by the U.S. Department of the Treasury. And, what would be the size of this yet another "elephant in the room"? Well, for Fiscal Year 2017, "Agency

Debt" was reportedly about **$8.86 trillion**; and in Fiscal Year 2018 it is projected to increase to about **$9.26 trillion**.

As noted in the quotation at the beginning of this Section, Thomas Jefferson (1743–1826) considered the **"public debt"** to be the **"greatest danger to our independence."** His being a highly-qualified and not-to-taken-lightly view, considering that Jefferson was one of our country's Founding Fathers; the principal author of our Declaration of Independence in 1776; our third U.S. President; a passionate spokesman for democracy; our first U.S. Secretary of State under President Washington; organizer of the Democratic-Republican Party; and with worldwide influence, supported the rights of the individual.

Furthermore, given the massive, out-of-control, and clearly unsustainable nature of today's National Debt, Jefferson's concerns about the dangers of public debt were not only founded in much wisdom and experience. But also, with an abundance of prophetic (predictive) insight.

Whether considering the obligations reported as our **U.S. National Debt**, or the unsupported promises entailed in our **U.S. Unfunded Liabilities**, or so-called **Agency Debt**, all are in fact **"debt obligations"** that cannot be just wished or ignored away.

And in keeping with the many realities of life, there "will be" a day of reckoning on this subject. That is, the time when those from whom money has been borrowed, and those to whom money and benefits related promises have been made, will expect and demand fulfillment of those obligations. Regardless of the consequences; regardless of how painful or widespread the sacrifice and suffering.

At the beginning of this Section it was noted that, "historically speaking, a national debt has been a part of our country since its beginning." However, what has not been a part of our great nation until recent years is, for example, a nation being ravaged by "political correctness" – which, simply defined, is "denial of truth and reality." And, a nation more and more divided into groups that see themselves as "the victims," and groups that are being viewed and treated as "the oppressors." With "the victims" behaving like they are "owed" food, shelter, healthcare, entertainment, and every other want and need they identify. And, "the oppressors" of course being anyone not in agreement with the views and demands of "the victims."

Furthermore, what has also not always been a part of our once much prouder and more responsible nation, is a federal government of ever-growing magnitude (re: the "Eight-Page Listing of Federal Government Agencies" included on pages 67-74). And, what has also not always been so widespread and nation destructive engrained, is the extent of voters willing to selfishly vote themselves unjustified benefits from the public treasury, and, politicians willing to selfishly use the public treasury to bribe voters in order to achieve or retain their positions of political power and personal gain.

And, our nation's history has not until more recent years included giving countless and often untrackable millions of illegal aliens access to our public treasury by way of housing, food stamps, healthcare, and other benefits—paid for by an America already in irresponsible debt.

Of course the above examples are but a limited few of a growing many of the contributors to our out of control National Debt. An unsustainable debt that, on our nation's present course, is shamefully being passed to today's young children, grandchildren, and the not yet born.

= = =

"The American Republic will endure until the day Congress discovers that it can bribe the public with the public's money."
–Alexis De Tocqueville (1805-1859)

"The consequences arising from the continual accumulation of public debts in other countries ought to admonish us to be careful to prevent their growth in our own." – John Adams (1735-1826), First U.S. Vice President; Second U.S. President. [Words from his First Address to Congress, November 23, 1797]

"I would vote against raising the national debt ceiling. Again, this is about mortgaging the future of unborn generations of Americans. It's a form of taxation without representation. I don't think we can do that." – Mike Lee (1971-), U.S. Senator from Utah

"Grasping the Size" of a $21 Trillion Debt!

> *"A wise and frugal government… shall restrain men from injuring one another, shall leave them otherwise free to regulate their own pursuits of industry and improvement, and shall not take from the mouth of labor the bread it has earned. This is the sum of good government."* – *Thomas Jefferson* **(1743–1826), 3rd U.S. President.** **[Words from his** *First Inaugural Address, March 4, 1801]*

It is highly likely that none among us can truly grasp the size of **"one trillion" (1,000,000,000,000)** of anything, let alone **"twenty-one trillion"!** Even with the aid of the many professionally-developed charts and graphic examples available through a growing number of web-sites and other sources. Sources this writer encourages the review of, and some of which are identified in the herein Section titled, *References and Recommended Readings.*

However, until choosing to benefit from such material, the few relatively simplified examples inserted below should serve as meaningful eye-openers to the truly staggering and unsustainable nature of our **$21 trillion National Debt**.

But first, a few explanatory words about the numbers included in this Section and elsewhere throughout this book.

Naturally, all data relating to our National Debt is constantly undergoing rapid change. And, by the time this book is published, many if not most of the numerical values identified herein will of course have changed, and generally, very dramatically so.

Furthermore, there seems to be no notable evidence that those with a craving for detail and having perfectionist leanings are staying up nights and engaged in related public protests about our government's irresponsible spending. So, the likelihood that some of the intentionally generalized information presented herein might by chance be "off" by a dollar, inch, mile, year, second, cubic foot, etc., or so, shouldn't be all that grievous or otherwise unaccepting. Nor, should such potential numbers glitches detract in any meaningful way from the truly serious message intended by this writing.

Now, for a few examples of just how enormous and out of control our **$21 Trillion National Debt** truly is:

(1.) **$21 Trillion Dollars = $21,000,000,000,000 (or 21 million million)**.

(2.) The circumference of (distance around) the Earth is about **24,901** miles. A U.S. one dollar bill is 6.14 inches long. Lining up **21 trillion U.S. one dollar bills** lengthways would circle the Earth about **81,725** times.

(3.) A round-trip from the Earth to the planet Saturn and back would be about **1.66 billion miles**. Lining up **21 trillion U.S. one dollar bills lengthways** would reach more than **2.03 billion miles**, or well beyond a round trip from the Earth to Saturn and back.

(4.) With a volume of more than **472 million cubic feet**, the Boeing Everett factory in the state of Washington is reportedly the world's largest building.   About **837.4 million cubic feet of space** would be needed to store **$21 trillion** — or a building about **1.8 times the size** of Boeing's huge facility.

(5.) To pay back **$21 trillion**, at a rate of one dollar per second, would take about **665,905 years**.

(6.) For a shameful period of time, our federal government has been **overspending** about **$1 trillion** in **new debt** each year. If a "very generous" taxpayer earning about $50,000 per year decided to use "all" of his or her income — to pay-off just the principal (not including interest) of one year of **new debt** — it would take **20 million years** to do so. Paying-off just the principal of our **total debt of $21 trillion** would take **420 million years**.

(7.) However, if we were to divide our $21 trillion National Debt between the estimated 121 million or so U.S. income taxpayers that are still left, the principal of $21 trillion could be wiped out in about **3.5 years**. But, again, this assumes each income taxpayer earned about $50,000 per year and would use "all" of their income for payment of this debt, and spend nothing on anything else, including food, shelter, clothing, transportation, healthcare, or entertainment, etc.!

Now, with the above examples of how truly massive our **$21 trillion National Debt** is, try as you may to mentally grasp the size of "the real elephant in the room"—an estimated **$112 trillion of U.S. Unfunded Liabilities**!

In the end, no matter how diced, sliced, or otherwise depicted, our **U.S. National Debt** and **Unfunded Liabilities** are mammoth obligation monsters that will not just go away. Regardless of how deep we bury our heads in the sands of distraction, apathy, complacency, denial, and greed.

= = =

"Our national debt is our biggest national security threat." — *Admiral Mike Mullen (1946-), Retired. [Statement, June 24, 2012}*

"Not only is our out-of-control debt fiscally irresponsible, it's unethical to put that debt on the backs of the next generation. It's time to get serious ..." — Dave Brat (1964-), U.S. Representative from Virginia

The "Interest" on Our National Debt

The "Interest" on our National Debt is simply (or should be simply) how much our federal government must pay to holders of its debt each year. However, as you will see within this Section, how our federal government determines, manages, and reports such interest is anything but "simple."

As noted in the following Table, the "interest" on our National Debt is becoming a bigger and bigger part of federal government spending. Consuming, for example, **$310 billion** (about 7.4 percent) of the Federal Budget for Fiscal Year 2018 (October 1, 2017 through September 30, 2018). Making "Interest on our National Debt" among the largest budget items. Exceeded only by budget items such as: Social Security benefits ($987 billion); Military spending ($874.4 billion); Medicare spending ($582 billion); and Medicaid spending ($400 billion).

<u>Actual</u> & Projected Interest Expense on "Public Debt" Portion of U.S. National Debt (Fiscal Years 2008 – 2028)

Fiscal Year	Interest on the Debt (Billion)	Interest Rate on 10-Year Treasury	Public Debt (Billion)	Percent of Budget
<u>2008</u>	$253	3.7%	$5,803	8.5%
<u>2009</u>	$187	3.3%	$7,545	5.3%
<u>2010</u>	$196	3.2%	$9,019	5.7%
<u>2011</u>	$230	2.8%	$10,128	6.4%
<u>2012</u>	$220	1.8%	$11,281	6.2%
<u>2013</u>	$221	2.4%	$11,983	6.4%
<u>2014</u>	$229	2.5%	$12,780	6.5%
<u>2015</u>	$223	2.1%	$13,117	6.0%
<u>2016</u>	$240	1.8%	$14,168	6.2%
<u>2017</u>	$263	2.7%	$14,824	6.8%
<u>2018</u>	$310	2.6%	$15,790	7.4%
2019	$363	3.1%	$16,872	8.2%
2020	$447	3.4%	$17,947	9.7%
2021	$510	3.6%	$18,950	10.7%
2022	$568	3.7%	$19,946	11.4%
2023	$619	3.7%	$20,809	12.0%
2024	$658	3.7%	$21,495	12.4%
2025	$688	3.7%	$22,137	12.5%
2026	$717	3.6%	$22,703	12.5%
2027	$740	3.6%	$23,194	12.4%
2028	$761	3.6%	$23,684	12.2%

(Sources: "Historical Tables, Table 3-1, Office of Management and Budget, FY 2019 Budget, Office of Management and Budget, February 12, 2018.)

Furthermore, it is important to note that the **"Interest on the Debt"** shown in the above Table **"applies only"** to the **"Public**

Debt" portion of our National Debt. While, as also noted in previous Sections of this writing, our National Debt is actually made up of the combination of the following "two" broad categories:

(1.) ***Public Debt***:   This is money our federal government borrows from American investors; foreign investors; foreign governments; etc., through the sale of U.S. Treasury Bills, Notes, and Bonds; U.S. Savings Bonds; etc.

In 2018, this Public Debt portion amounted to about $15.8 trillion (about 75 percent of the total National Debt).

(2.) ***Intra-governmental Debt:*** This is money our federal government owes itself. Such as money borrowed from the Social Security and Medicare trust funds; Military Retirement funds; Civil Service funds; Federal Reserve Banks; etc.

In 2018, this Intra-governmental Debt portion amounted to about $5.2 trillion (about 25 percent of the total National Debt).

However, it seems our federal government considers **"Intra-governmental Debt"** to be debt that our federal government so-called **"owes itself."** As a result, the payment of interest to such accounts is considered an "intra-governmental transaction" that (supposedly) has no effect on net interest payments or on the budget deficit. And so, such "Intra-governmental Debt" is typically **not** included in various government reporting of interest expense on our National Debt. *[Good luck with trying to apply such practices on your next state and federal income tax return, home budget, home mortgage, etc.]*

According to 2018 projections by the Office of the Management and Budget, interest rates are expected to rise to above 3 percent in 2019, and thereafter increase to 3.7 percent by **2025**.

By then, the **interest on the "public portion"** of our U.S. National debt will be about **$688 billion**, and take up 12.5 percent of the federal budget.

Furthermore, if current federal government tax and spend policies remain in effect, some forecasts indicate that **"Interest"** payments on our U.S. National Debt could well exceed **$1 trillion by 2028**.

And, according to estimates by the Committee for a Responsible Federal Budget (CRFB), a fiscal watchdog group, an interest expense in that range would amount to about 3.6 percent of our entire U.S. economy.

In this senior-citizen writer's view, the above potential of a **$1 trillion yearly interest payment** on our National Debt is not far-fetched or otherwise unrealistic. Since, for example, in **July 1974**, the month and year my wife Ann and I signed our first home mortgage, the **U.S. Prime Interest Rate was "12 percent."**

And, in rough numbers, a 12 percent interest rate applied to, for example, even our as-of-this-writing **2018 National Debt of $21 trillion**, would amount to a yearly interest payment of about **$1.9 trillion**! Representing, by any realistic standard, a nation-threatening economic disaster.

As noted at the beginning of this Section—how our federal government determines, manages, and reports interest regarding our National Debt is anything but "simple."

= = =

"As an individual who undertakes to live by borrowing, soon finds his original means devoured by interest, and next no one left to borrow from--so must it be with a government."
— Abraham Lincoln (1809-1865), 16th U.S. President

"I think it's clear, if you do simple arithmetic, that the fiscal path that the nation is on is simply not sustainable." — Erskine Bowles (1945-), Co-chair, National Commission on Fiscal Responsibility

"I'm concerned that our increasing fractious political process, particularly with respect to federal spending, is threatening our ability to properly defend our nation both in the short term and especially in the long term." "The failure to address our long term fiscal situation has increased the national debt to over \$20 trillion and growing." "I would urge all of us to recognize the need to address this challenge and to take action as soon as possible before a fiscal crisis occurs that truly undermines our ability to ensure our national security." – Dan Coats (1943-), Director of U.S. National Intelligence since 2017. [Words from his testimony before U.S. Senate Select Committee on Intelligence hearing on worldwide threats, February 13, 2018]

Who Owns
Our National Debt?

As earlier noted and warrants repeating, "ownership" of our **National Debt** primarily falls into two broad categories:

(1.) *Public Debt*: Money our federal government borrows from American investors; foreign investors; foreign governments; etc., through the sale of U.S. Treasury Bills, Notes, and Bonds; U.S. Savings Bonds; etc.

(2.) *Intra-governmental Debt:* Money our federal government owes itself. Such as money borrowed from the Social Security and Medicare trust funds; Military Retirement funds; Civil Service funds; Federal Reserve Banks; etc.

While all aspects of our National Debt undergo constant change, the following **Tables** provide a more detail example of ownership, based on our at that time **$20.2 trillion National Debt**, as reported on **September 30, 2017**, by the White House Office of Management and Budget (OMB) for **Fiscal Year 2017**:

(Re: OMB Reporting—Fiscal Year 2017)

Amount (Trillions)	Type	Portion of Total
$14.7	Publicly Held Debt	72%
$5.6	Intragovernmental Debt	28%

Ownership	Amount (Billions)	Portion of Total
Public Debt - *(Foreign-Owned)*	**$6,302**	**31%**
China	$1,182	6%
Japan	$1,096	5%
Ireland	$311	2%
Brazil	$273	1%
Cayman Islands	$247	1%
United Kingdom	$237	1%
Switzerland	$253	1%
Luxembourg	$214	1%
Hong Kong	$194	1%
Taiwan	$184	1%
Other Nations	$2,110	10%
Public Debt – *(Domestic, Non-Federal)*	**$5,885**	**29%**
Mutual Funds	$1,651	8%
State & Local Governments	$697	3%
Banks & Savings Institutions	$605	3%
Private Pension Funds	$531	3%
Insurance Companies	$343	2%
State & Local Government Pension Funds	$216	1%

(Continued on following page)

(Continued from previous page)

Ownership	Amount (Billions)	Portion of Total
Public Debt - *(Domestic, Non-Federal)* - *(Continued)*		
U.S. Savings Bond Holders	$162	1%
Other Investors	$1,680	8%
Public Debt - *(Federal Reserve)*	**$2,465**	**12%**
Intragovernmental Debt	**$5,571**	**28%**
Social Security	$2,890	14%
Civil Service Retirement and Disability	$894	4%
Military Retirement	$661	3%
Medicare	$268	1%
Department of Defense Retiree Healthcare	$226	1%
Postal Service Retiree Healthcare	$49	0%
Other Funds	$583	3%
Total "Public" & "Intragovernmental" Debt:	**$20,224**	**100%**

There are several important takeaways from this Section. Such as: (1.) the inconceivable size and wide spread nature of our National Debt; (2.) like interest on the debt, tracking and reporting of ownership is likewise anything but simple; and,

(3.) the notable fact that the largest holder of our National Debt is not a foreign government, such as China, Japan, etc., but rather, our nation's "Social Security" Trust Account.

Furthermore, we must never forget that it is "we the people" who are ultimately responsible for our National Debt. Therefore, we must not allow ourselves to be misled or distracted by words and expressions such as "government held"; "the government borrows"; "the government owes;" "the government pays"; or other use of terms that seemingly detach us from this out of control and unsustainable menace to future generations of Americans.

= = =

"I place economy among the first and most important virtues, and public debt as the greatest of dangers to be feared. To preserve our independence, we must not let our rulers load us with perpetual debt. If we run into such debts, we must be taxed in our meat and drink, in our necessities and in our comforts, in our labor and in our amusements." – Thomas Jefferson (1743-1826), a U.S. Founding Father; principal author of the Declaration of Independence; 3rd U.S. President

More About "Intra-governmental Debt"

[This Section is meant to serve as a special supplement to the previous Section titled "Who Owns Our National Debt?"]

As earlier noted, the **Public Debt** portion of our National Debt is basically money our federal government borrows from American investors; foreign investors; foreign governments; etc., through the sale of U.S. Treasury Bills, Notes, and Bonds; U.S. Savings Bonds; etc.

Whereas, the **Intra-governmental Debt** portion of our National Debt is money our federal government "so-called" owes itself. Such as money borrowed from the Social Security and Medicare trust funds; Military Retirement funds; Civil Service funds; Federal Reserve Banks; etc.

As such, **Intra-governmental Debt** is money typically owed to some 230 or more federal government agencies. Agencies that have the Congress-established requirement or authority to invest excess receipts (money) in special U.S. Treasury securities. For example, when Social Security or other agencies such as shown below take in more money from payroll taxes than they have to presently pay out in benefits.

- **Social Security Administration** — which has control of the "Federal Old Age and Survivors Insurance Trust Fund"; "Federal Disability Insurance Trust Fund"; etc.

- **Office of Personnel Management** — which has control of the "Civil Service Retirement and Disability Fund"; "Postal Service Retiree Health Benefits Fund"; etc.

- **Department of Defense** — "Military Retirement Fund"; "DOD Medicare-Eligible Retiree Health Care Fund";

- **Department of Health and Human Services** — "Federal Supplementary Medical Insurance Trust Fund"; etc.

- etc.; etc.; etc.

In other words, federal agencies, such as the above, use excess (not yet spent) money from funds they control to invest in (purchase) U.S. Treasury securities. Securities that are guaranteed for principal and interest by the full faith and credit of the U.S. Government—which of course is ultimately "we the people."

In the meantime, what happens to money passed, for example, from the Social Security Trust Fund to the U.S. Treasury to purchase Treasury securities?

Well, it gets spent by Congress to pay for more and more promises made to us, in an effort to assure our votes and maintain positions of political power, influence, and other self-benefit.

Therefore, **Intra-governmental Debt** is much more than just an accounting transaction between two federal government agencies. Much more than our federal government "so-called" borrowing from and only owing itself.

To the contrary, in continuing with the above example, a hole (debt) has been left in the U.S. Treasury. A yet to be paid back debt to, for example, the Social Security Trust Fund. And at some the point the Social Security Administration will have to cash in its prior purchased Treasury Securities to pay benefits. But the cash to pay this debt has been spent on other promises and will have to come from somewhere else.

Therefore, to fill the resulting hole (debt) left in the U.S. Treasury, one or more of the following measures must at some point be taken: **(1.)** Congress increase taxes; **(2.)** Congress cut federal spending; and/or **(3.)** the Treasury issue more debt (print more money). Each of which involve an array of complexities and consequences, many of which are purposefully not addressed by this limited writing.

Of course there are other options. For example, keep kicking the can of responsibility down the road until "someone else" has to ultimately refuse or otherwise fail to honor future Social Security, Veterans, and/or other promised benefits, etc.

"All the perplexities, confusion and distress in America arise not from defects in the Constitution or Confederation, not from a want of honor or virtue so much as from downright ignorance of the nature of coin, credit and circulation." – John Adams (1735-1826), a U.S. Founding Father; First U.S. Vice President; Second U.S. President. [Words from the Constitutional Convention (1787)]

The Most Recent "Balanced" Federal Budget

> *"The trouble with Socialism is that eventually you run out of other people's money."* — *Margaret Thatcher (1925-2013), Prime Minister of the United Kingdom from 1979-1990*

(Source: CBS News; Fox News; U.S. CBO)

Reportedly, the last "balanced" federal budgets were in fiscal years 1998, 1999, 2000, and 2001 — when Democrat Bill Clinton was president, and the Republicans controlled Congress. The Republican-controlled Congress approved the appropriations for each one of those years and Democratic President Bill Clinton signed them. When President Clinton governed with a Democrat-controlled Congress, in fiscal years 1994 and 1995, the federal government reportedly ran deficits of $203.2 billion and $163.9 billion respectively.

However, some have argued that President Clinton and Congress were not totally up-front about the nature of the reported balanced budgets. Critics claiming that, while the official numbers (which included "off-budget" items including the Social Security trust funds) did show surpluses for all four fiscal years of Clinton's second term . . . the "on-budget" totals alone showed a different view. That being, only the 1999 and 2000 fiscal years recorded on-budget surpluses.

Therefore, over the years 1998 to 2001 the total surplus may have added up to only about $26 billion. And, furthermore, since most of the surplus was calculated from money flowing into the Social Security trust funds, **the National Debt didn't actually get paid-down during the sum of these four years, but instead increased $280 billion or more**.

"Fuzzy numbers" such as you have just read are of course hard, if not impossible, to grasp, track, and determine accountability for. And, that's no doubt just the way our ever growing and out of control federal government has planned and wishes it to be! As demonstrated by our National Debt continuing to dramatically increase, and government spending continues to exceed income (i.e., tax revenues).

For example, during the eight-year administration of President George W. Bush our National Debt almost doubled—to $5.7 trillion. And, despite this massive increase over Bush's eight years, President Obama amassed more National Debt in his first five years than all previous presidents combined.

Overall, between Bush and Obama our National Debt more than *quadrupled* in size! As policies in place during and at the end of President Obama's administration, projected our National Debt to increase another 50 percent over the next 10 years, then rapidly rise thereafter! A shameful projection obviously on track, given our 2018 National Debt of $21 trillion.

That is, unless President Trump's Make America Great Again agenda, and the support of "we the people," include some way of dramatically reversing this nation destroying trend.

=   =   =

"The real goal should be reduced government spending, rather than balanced budgets achieved by ever rising tax rates to cover ever rising spending."   — Thomas Sowell (1930-), an American economist and social theorist; Senior Fellow at the Hoover Institution, Stanford University

"At what point will Washington throw in the towel and stop mortgaging the future of our children and grandchildren -- when interest on national debt exceeds total annual revenues or when lending countries lose confidence in our ability to repay our debt?" – Edward Inghrim (1943-2017). [Words from "The national debt is even worse than you think", Lehigh Valley Live, March 20, 2017]

Where Our Tax Dollars Go

According to the Congressional Budget Office (CBO), it is expected that the federal budget for fiscal year 2018 (October 2017 through September 2018) will be about **$4.09 trillion**.

However, tax revenue for same period is expected to only be about **$3.5 trillion**. About half of this $3.5 trillion comes from individual income taxes; about one-third from payroll taxes (which includes Social Security and Medicare taxes); and the remaining from corporate and other taxes.

Of course, a budget (projected spending) of **$4.09 trillion** against tax revenues of only **$3.5 trillion**, leaves a deficit (shortage) of more than **$560 billion**. A shortage that must be covered by actions such as borrowing which adds to our National Debt, or by printing more money which ultimately decreases the value of our U.S. dollar.

The Table below provides a relatively recent example of where our tax dollars are being spent. Note, however, that at the time of this April 2018 writing, the latest data available from the Congressional Budget Office (CBO) was from its June 2017 report. Which was published prior to the December 2017 enacted tax cut and the budget deal subsequently reached in February 2018. Therefore, the values shown below are based on 2017 CBO projections.

U.S Federal Budget (Fiscal Year 2018)

Source: Congressional Budget Office (CBO) June 2017 Report

Category	Amount	Percent
Social Security	$988 billion	24.2%
Medicare	$711 billion	17.4%
Defense	$634 billion	15.5%
Medicaid	$410 billion	10.0%
Interest on National Debt	$310 billion	7.6%
Income Security Programs	$292 billion	7.1%
Federal Civilian & Military Retirement	$160 billion	3.9%
Veterans' Programs	$101 billion	2.5%
Agriculture & Other Programs	$84 billion	2.1%
Children's' Health Insurance Program (CHIP) & Subsidies for Affordable Care Act	$74 billion	1.8%
Other	$326 billion	7.9%
Total:	$4.09 trillion	100%

Even at today's historically low interest rates, in reviewing the above Table, note that FY 2018 "Interest on our National Debt" is about half our spending on "Defense."

The Table below provides a comparison of recent Federal Government Spending to that of years past. Note the dramatic upward trend in spending for Social Programs as compared to the other listed categories.

U.S. Federal Spending (Period 1960-2016)
Source: U.S. Office of Management and Budget (OMB)

	Category	Portion of Federal Spending						
		1960	1970	1980	1990	2000	2010	2016
1.	Social Programs	21%	32%	45%	44%	54%	61%	63%
2.	National Defense	53%	42%	26%	25%	19%	20%	18%
3.	General Government & Debt Service	19%	18%	21%	25%	21%	13%	14%
4.	Economic Affairs & Infrastructure	6%	7%	7%	5%	5%	4%	4%
5.	Public Order & Safety	0%	0%	1%	1%	1%	1%	1%

(1.) <u>Social Programs</u>: Include income security, healthcare, education, housing, and recreation.

(2.) <u>National defense</u>: Includes military spending and veterans' benefits.

(3.) <u>General Government & Debt Service</u>: Includes the executive & legislative branches, tax collection, financial management, and interest payments.

(Continued on next page)

(4.) _**Economic Affairs & Infrastructure:**_ Includes transportation, general economic & labor affairs, agriculture, natural resources, energy, and space. (This excludes spending for infrastructure projects such as new highways, which is not accounted for in above Table.)

(5.) _**Public Order & Safety:**_ Includes police, fire, law courts, prisons, and immigration enforcement.

In reviewing the above Office of Management and Budget (OMB) data, it should be noted that the "Income Security" identified in footnote "(1.) _Social Programs_" is a range of programs, providing cash or near-cash assistance (such as: housing, nutrition, and energy assistance) to low-income persons, and benefits to certain retirees, persons with disabilities, and the unemployed.

Housing assistance programs account for the largest share of discretionary funding in this "Income Security" category. Followed by major federal entitlement programs such as, unemployment insurance, trade adjustment assistance income support, food stamps, Temporary Assistance to Needy Families, foster care, and Supplemental Security Income. With federal and other retirement and disability programs making up about one third of the funds in this category.

= = =

After considering the various categories of federal government spending depicted by the examples within this Section, take a realistic wild guess where the "big cuts" will have to eventually come from. That is, when the "day of reckoning" arrives on our out-of-control and unsustainable U.S. National Debt and Unfunded Liabilities.

As another example of where our tax dollars go, pages 67 through 74 include an **"Eight-page listing" of some 438 Federal Government Agencies**. An ever-growing maze of "agencies" identified under a broad mix of terms and titles, such as: Agencies, Bureaus, Commissions, Departments, Services, Offices, Boards, Corporations, Foundations, Administrations, Councils, Divisions, etc., etc. A practice especially helpful in making it difficult, if not impossible, to track ultimate responsibility; accountability; and outdated or duplicated functions, etc. Agencies most of which are staffed with unelected bureaucrats who are driven to seek and spend funding that justifies their existence. Overall, a self-perpetuating bureaucracy that substantially adds to and further complicates efforts to bring our nation's debt under control.

= = =

"My reading of history convinces me that most bad government results from too much government." –Thomas Jefferson (1743-1826), a U.S. Founding Father; principal author of the Declaration of Independence; 3rd U.S. President

"In general, the art of government consists of taking as much money as possible from one party of the citizens to give to the other."
– Voltaire (1694-1778), a French Enlightenment writer; historian; philosopher

"A government which robs Peter to pay Paul can always depend on the support of Paul." — George Bernard Shaw (1856-1950), an Irish playwright; critic; polemicist; political activist

"We don't have a trillion-dollar debt because we haven't taxed enough; we have a trillion-dollar debt because we spend too much." — Ronald Reagan (1911-2004), 40th U.S. President

"It took the national debt two hundred years to reach $1 trillion. Supply Side Economics quadrupled the national debt to over $4 trillion in twelve years (1980-1992) under the Republicans. Bill Clinton actually paid down the national debt. How did he do it? He raised taxes. It produced the longest sustained economic expansion in U.S. History." — Ed Schultz (1954-), American television/radio host; political commentator; former sports broadcaster

"Back in 2008, candidate Obama called a $10 trillion national debt 'unpatriotic' - serious talk from what looked to be a serious reformer. Yet by his own decisions, President Obama has added more debt than any other president before him, and more than all the troubled governments of Europe combined. One president, one term, $5 trillion in new debt." — Paul Ryan (1970-), 54th Speaker of the U.S. House of Representatives since 2015

Social Security Deficits are "Permanent & Growing"

The Social Security "trust funds" are financial accounts in the U.S. Treasury. There are two separate Social Security trust funds. The Old-Age and Survivors Insurance (OASI) Trust Fund pays retirement and survivors benefits, and the Disability Insurance (DI) Trust Fund pays disability benefits.

Social Security is now the biggest share of the Federal Government Budget, and in 2018 is expected to pay out about $988 billion in benefits.

Social Security is presently funded through a 6.2 percent payroll tax that workers pay and by another 6.2 percent that employers pay for each worker. Self-employed persons have to pay the full 12.4 percent.

All of America's employees and their families—past, present, and future—have a stake in our Social Security program. The retirement safety net signed into law in 1935 by then President Roosevelt. A thereafter source of post-work income for countless Americans over the decades since.

However, the future of Social Security is now very uncertain. For example, as stressed in the 2017 annual report of the Board of Trustees of the Social Security Trust Funds—Social Security's income is expected to exceed its expenses only until about 2021. The same report estimates that by about 2034 the reserves (balance left) in both Security Trust Funds will be depleted. And without "reforms" (such as more taxes and less benefits), each year after 2034 it is projected that annual Social Security taxes will only cover about 75 percent of Social Security benefits due.

And then along comes a June 6, 2018 Associated Press (AP) published article, titled **"Medicare finances worsening,"** which reads in part:

"Medicare will run out of money sooner than expected, and Social Security's financial problems can't be ignored either, the government said Tuesday (June 5, 2018) in a sobering checkup on programs vital to the middle class. The report from program trustees says Medicare will become insolvent in 2026 — three years earlier than previously forecasted. Its giant trust fund for inpatient care won't be able to fully cover projected medical bills starting at that point. The report says Social Security will become insolvent in 2034 — no change from the projection last year (2017). The warning serves as a reminder of major issues left to languish while Washington plunges deeper into partisan strife. Demands on both

programs (Social Security and Medicare) are increasing as America ages. Unless lawmakers act, both programs face the prospect of being unable to cover the full cost of promised benefits. Medicare provides health insurance for about 60 million people, most of whom are age 65 and older. More than 62 million retirees, disabled workers, spouses and surviving children receive Social Security. . . ."

A critical factor in Social Security's uncertain future is of course the dramatic increase in the number of adults 65 and older. For example, starting in January 2011, more than 10,000 Americans from the "Baby Boomers" generation began turning 65 "each day"! A pattern that will continue until about 2030. *[The "Baby Boomers" being the approximately 77 million Americans born during time frame of 1946 through 1965.]*

While there is little disagreement about the Social Security system being in serious financial trouble, there remains much debate about what needs to be done to fix it. Nevertheless, in the end, common sense and a grasp of reality will likely dictate that any meaningful fix include, increased taxes, reduced benefits, and appropriately shared sacrifice. Hopefully brought about through likewise appropriately shared responsibility on the part of both present and future generations of Americans.

= = =

"And this is why our ever-growing national debt is so perilous -- because even those who believe as I do that a strong and ready defense is the cornerstone of our security won't be able to guarantee it if current fiscal trends persist. Put simply: if we do nothing to pay down this debt and address the needs of Social Security, Medicare, and Medicaid, then America risks finding itself so weakened financially that someday in the not-too-distant future we just won't have the resources we need to equip and maintain our forces in the places they're needed most." — Mitch McConnell (1942-), Senior *U.S. Senator from Kentucky; U.S. Senate Majority Leader since January 3, 2015. [Words are his on the Senate floor, United States Congressional Record, July 23, 2009]*

"In a 1789 letter to his friend James Madison, Thomas Jefferson raised the philosophical and moral question of whether 'one generation of men has a right to bind another.' He believed the answer was no, 'that the earth belongs in usufruct to the living.' He believed it a principle of 'very extensive application and consequence, in every country.' Applying it to government borrowing, he argued that it was unjust and unrepublican for one generation of a nation to encumber the next with the obligation to discharge the debts of the first. After all, the following generation cannot have given their consent to decisions made by their fathers, nor will have they have necessarily benefited from the deficit expenditures." — H.A. Scott Trask, Historian. Re: Perpetual Debt: *From the British Empire to the American Hegemon. January 27, 2004*

Will Our National Debt Ever Be Paid-Off?

Will our $21 trillion (and growing) U.S. National Debt ever be paid-off? And, will the obligations that make up our $112 trillion (and growing) U.S. Unfunded Liabilities ever be honored? The realistic answer to both of these questions is, "highly likely no!"

Of course, the answer to "Why not?" rests in large part in the self-destructive sides of human nature. More specifically, in the wide-spread ignorance, apathy, complacency, denial, and greed of "we the people." With "greed" being chief among the culprits.

Interwoven in the above is the fact that most (if not all) politics are in fact **"local."** In likeness to the view that "charity begins at home," and, "taxes and sacrifices are OK as long as they are endured by someone else," etc.

History supports the fact that many if not most politicians crave positions of power, influence, and otherwise self-fulfillment. As a result, they make monumental promises to get and remain elected. And when the taxpayer-funded public treasury lacks the money to backup those promises—on behalf of "we the people," our government continues to borrow and/or print more money.

Furthermore, halting the increase in our National Debt, and paying back borrowed funds means making difficult decisions and enduring sacrifices. Such as, spending cuts and/or tax increases, reduced benefits, etc. But, as earlier noted, we voters do not like tax increases, spending cuts, reduced benefits, etc.—unless of course they apply to someone else. Therefore politicians who want to get or remain elected will unrelentingly strive to avoid the political kiss of death associated with "more taxes," "reduced benefits," etc.

Therefore—in the short term—a much easier and more irresponsible path is just to keep spending the future of our nation's children. Yes, rather than endure the sacrifices required to halt reckless government spending and pay down our National Debt, we will likely just continue to take on more and more debt. And print more and more money backed up by less and less—which through inflation make the U.S. dollar (our money) worth less and less. And through money having less and less purchasing power, those to whom our U.S. debt is owed, will ultimately get back less and less than earlier promised—which is actually just another less obvious way of "defaulting on such debt."

And, so will continue the unsustainable debt death-spiral until the wheels eventually come off of our nation's wagon (so to speak).

That is, unless "we the people"—more specifically, the now "in charge" adults—are willing to put greed aside and demand that our federal government chart a more responsible path for our country. A new direction which, for example, acknowledges some of the more basic and vital realities of life. Such as: (1.) there is no such thing as "free"—because someone ultimately pays; (2.) the U.S. cannot, nor is it obligated to, feed, clothe, house, entertain, and provide medical care, etc., for the planet Earth; (3.) persons entering the U.S. illegally are "illegal aliens" and have no right of access to benefits from the public treasury; and (4.) adult U.S. citizens of able body and able mind have the right to pursue America's opportunities—not the right to a free ride on the public treasury.

Furthermore, our nation's critically needed and long past due new path must unrelentingly have as its not negotiable central aim—the assurance that our young children and grandchildren of today, and other future generations of Americans, will likewise have the opportunity to experience, enjoy, appreciate, protect, and pass on to future generations, an America of (God-given) Rights to life, liberty, and pursuit of happiness.

= = =

"The problem is real, and the solution will be painful. We must stabilize and then reduce the national debt, or we could spend $1 trillion a year in interest alone by 2020. There is no easy way out of our debt problem, so everything must be on the table. A sensible, realistic plan requires shared sacrifice – and Washington must lead the way and tighten its belt." – The Moment of Truth: Report of the National Commission on Fiscal Responsibility and Reform, The White House, December 1, 2010

"History is littered with examples of major economic and financial crises in countries that have engaged in public spending profligacy. That sad experience should be raising red flags in the United States, where the unsustainable longer-run trajectory of the US public finances is now suggesting the real risk of either a destructive burst of inflation or an outright government debt default. This is particularly the case in today's US context where an ever-increasing portion of the US budget deficit is being financed by foreigners and where entitlement programs threaten over the longer haul to compound an already highly compromised public finance position."
– Desmond Lachman, a resident Fellow at the American Enterprise Institute (AEI). Re: On the Fiscal Road to Serfdom, American Enterprise Institute. October 22, 2009

Where Do You & I Stand?

When it comes to our nation's National Debt and Unfunded Liabilities, most of us seem to fall into one of the following groups:

1. Those who just "tune out" the subjects altogether and bury their heads in the sand (or more fittingly put, "up their backside").

2. Those who refuse to accept or believe that our National Debt and Unfunded Liabilities actually exits.

3. Those who accept that our National Debt and Unfunded Liabilities do exist, but "BS" themselves into believing such debts and obligations don't really matter.

4. Those who accept that our National Debt and Unfunded Liabilities do exist, but "BS" themselves into believing that "the government" will somehow "fix things" (ignoring the

fact that "the government" of "we the people" is the cause of our nation's debt problem in the first place).

5. Those who accept that our National Debt and Unfunded Liabilities do exist, and that such are a real problem, but are willing to kick the can of responsibility down the road for future generations of Americans to deal with. And with same attitude are able to look America's young children and grandchildren in the eye, and sleep well at night.

6. Those who view our nation's National Debt and Unfunded Liabilities in rational and level-headed manner, and understand that unsustainable debts of such magnitude will one day result in disastrous economic consequences of unimaginable nature and extent. And with such view strive to make sensible personal preparations for such outcome.

7. Those who view our nation's National Debt and Unfunded Liabilities in rational and level-headed manner, and understand that unsustainable debts of such magnitude will one day result in disastrous economic consequences of unimaginable nature and extent. And with such view, not only strive to make sensible personal preparations for such outcome. But, also through the power of their vote and other means available to them, unrelentingly demand systematic elimination of the threats posed by our National Debt and Unfunded Liabilities. Through responsible government tax and spend legislation, policies, procedures, and budgeting.

And so, the crucial question remains—where do you and I stand?

In the end, our answers of course will determine whether we—the now so-called adults in charge—responsibly carry out our citizen-duty. Or, instead, choose to leave our young children and grandchildren of today, and America's generations not yet born, a shameful liberty-threatening legacy of unsustainable debt and unfulfilled promises.

= = =

"Those who stand for nothing fall for anything."
— Alexander Hamilton (1757-1804)

"You cannot escape the responsibility of tomorrow by evading it today." — Abraham Lincoln (1809-1865)

*"It was by the sober sense of our citizens that we were safely and steadily conducted **from monarchy** to republicanism, and it is by the same agency alone we can be kept from falling back."*
— Thomas Jefferson (1723-1826)

"Debt itself has become institutionalized. Today, many people simply accept as a fact of life that the national debt is unimaginably high. The problem, though, is that we cannot continue the exponential expansion of debt without a catastrophic economic outcome." — *Addison Wiggin (1968 -), American financial writer, publisher, and filmmaker. Re: The Demise of the Dollar*

Our
Constitutional Republic

"A [pure] democracy is nothing more than mob rule, where fifty-one percent of the people may take away the rights of the other forty-nine." – Thomas Jefferson (1743-1826)

"The mob is the mother of tyrants." – Diogenes (412BC-323BC)

Most alarmingly, a growing number of Americans know very little about the history, nature, and importance of our unique form of government. Unaware, for example, that there is sound reason why our United States Pledge of Allegiance refers to our country as a *Republic* and why our Declaration of Independence and Constitution do not mention the word *democracy*.

Our country's founders were very aware of the failures of prior democracies, such as ancient Athens and Rome. They feared creating a government having too many similarities to a *pure democracy*. They especially recognized the importance of ensuring the right of political dissent and protecting minority groups and individuals from the *tyranny of the majority*. They knew that a *pure democracy* could result in *mob rule*, where fifty-one percent of the people could take away the rights of the other forty-nine. Through their experience, insight, and great wisdom, they put in place a one-of-its-kind *constitutional republic* — **not** a *pure democracy*.

In so doing they passed to us a very special form of government where sovereignty deliberately rests with *we the people.* Where we may act on our own or through our elected representatives to deal with issues, where our government is a servant of its people — *where our government's power comes from and is limited by its citizens.* That is, until we further screw-it-up by irresponsibly continuing to give up our U.S. citizens' Constitution-guaranteed power to an ever-growing government loaded with self-serving, self-perpetuating, power and influence craving officials!

Our *Constitutional Republic* does include some likeness to a *democracy*, such as our use of democratic processes to elect our representatives, pass new laws, etc. But, as opposed to a democracy, our U.S. Constitution *limits* our government's power and spells out how our government is to be structured. As a result, our Constitutional Republic is divided into three separate but equal branches of government. The <u>Executive</u> (*Presidency*), <u>Legislative</u> (*Congress*), and <u>Judicial</u> (*Courts*). Our Constitution establishes that no branch has absolute power, therefore providing special checks and balances on our government system and protection for the rule of law.

Our Constitution is the life-blood of our Constitutional Republic. The foundation of this land of unequaled opportunity; best hope for mankind; and envy of countless people yet deprived of and seeking liberty. A liberty for which much sacrifice has been made by so many, and for which limitless measures must always be taken to defend, protect, and preserve!

Therefore, when seeking responsibility for the existence of, and resolution of, our U.S. National Debt and Unfunded Liabilities, and our nation's other ills, we ultimately need look no further than ourselves — "we the people."

= = =

"We may define a republic to be . . . a government which derives all its powers directly or indirectly from the great body of the people, and is administered by persons holding offices during pleasure for a limited period, or during good behavior."
—James Madison (1751-1836), a U.S. Founding Father; Fourth U.S. President

"But a Constitution of Government once changed from Freedom, can never be restored. Liberty, once lost, is lost forever."
—John Adams (1735-1826), a U.S. Founding Father; First U.S. Vice President; Second U.S. President

"To preserve our independence, we must not let our rulers load us with perpetual debt. We must make our election between economy and liberty, or profusion and servitude."
– *Thomas Jefferson (1743-1826), a U.S. Founding Father; principal author of the Declaration of Independence; 3rd U.S. President*

The "Lifespan" of Our Constitutional Republic?

> *"Pure democracies have ever been spectacles of turbulence and contention; have ever been found incompatible with personal security, or the rights of property; and have, in general, been as short in their lives as they have been violent in their deaths."*
> — *James Madison (1751-1836), 4th U.S. President*

It is important to note that the "life-cycle of a democracy" scenario included on the following page is an assertion of questionable origin. While nevertheless for years quoted and referenced by many, and long accessible in many forms through an array Internet sources and other media.

However, regardless of the scenario's origin, little open-minded consideration is needed to recognize some very unsettling similarities, between it and the dangerous path our **"Constitutional Republic"** has long been on. And any realistic comparison would find us very disturbingly somewhere around mid-point between Sequence 6 and 7. That is, a nation heavily consumed with *apathy* and dangerously deep into the even more self-destructive phase of *dependence*. Leaving *bondage* the next step in this scenario— towards loss of the precious liberty/freedom now often taken for granted and abused. A path that President Trump and constructive supporters of his "Make America Great Again" agenda are striving hard to reverse.

= = =

The Life Cycle of a Democracy

"A democracy cannot exist as a permanent form of government. It will continue until the voters discover they can vote themselves generous gifts from the public treasury. From that point on, the majority will always vote for the candidates who promise the most benefits from the public treasury. Eventually every democracy will collapse, due to loose fiscal policy, and be followed by a dictatorship. From the beginning, the greatest civilizations of the world have only lasted about 200 years, and have always progressed through the following sequence:

1. *From bondage to **spiritual faith**;*
2. *From spiritual faith to **great courage**;*
3. *From courage to **liberty**;*
4. *From liberty to **abundance**;*
5. *From abundance to **complacency**;*
6. *From complacency to **apathy**;*
7. *From apathy to **dependence**;*
8. *From dependence back to **bondage**."*

= = =

"The American Republic will endure until the day Congress discovers that it can bribe the public with the public's money."

—*Alexis De Tocqueville (1805-1859)*

Our U.S. "Bill of Rights"

*"We hold these truths to be self-Evident, that all men are created equal, that they are endowed by their Creator with certain unalienable Rights, that among these are **Life, Liberty and the pursuit of Happiness**. ---That to secure these rights, Governments are instituted among Men, deriving their just powers from the consent of the governed, ..."*

— The U.S. Declaration of Independence, 1776

The following is a transcription of the first ten amendments to our U.S. Constitution in their original form. These first ten amendments to the Constitution were ratified December 15, 1791, and form what is known as the "Bill of Rights."

Amendment I

Congress shall make no law respecting an establishment of religion, or prohibiting the free exercise thereof; or abridging the freedom of speech, or of the press; or the right of the people peaceably to assemble, and to petition the Government for a redress of grievances.

Amendment II

A well regulated Militia, being necessary to the security of a free State, the right of the people to keep and bear Arms, shall not be infringed.

Amendment III

No Soldier shall, in time of peace be quartered in any house, without the consent of the Owner, nor in time of war, but in a manner to be prescribed by law.

Amendment IV

The right of the people to be secure in their persons, houses, papers, and effects, against unreasonable searches and seizures, shall not be violated, and no Warrants shall issue, but upon probable cause, supported by Oath or affirmation, and particularly describing the place to be searched, and the persons or things to be seized.

Amendment V

No person shall be held to answer for a capital, or otherwise infamous crime, unless on a presentment or indictment of a Grand Jury, except in cases arising in the land or naval forces, or in the Militia, when in actual service in time of War or public danger; nor shall any person be subject for the same offence to be twice put in jeopardy of life or limb; nor shall be compelled in any criminal case to be a witness against himself, nor be deprived of life, liberty, or property, without due process of law; nor shall private property be taken for public use, without just compensation.

Amendment VI

In all criminal prosecutions, the accused shall enjoy the right to a speedy and public trial, by an impartial jury of the State and district wherein the crime shall have been committed, which district shall have been previously ascertained by law, and to be informed of the nature and cause of the accusation; to be confronted with the witnesses against him; to have compulsory process for obtaining witnesses in his favor, and to have the Assistance of Counsel for his defense.

Amendment VII

In Suits at common law, where the value in controversy shall exceed twenty dollars, the right of trial by jury shall be preserved, and no fact tried by a jury, shall be otherwise re-examined in any Court of the United States, than according to the rules of the common law.

Amendment VIII

Excessive bail shall not be required, nor excessive fines imposed, nor cruel and unusual punishments inflicted.

Amendment IX

The enumeration in the Constitution, of certain rights, shall not be construed to deny or disparage others retained by the people.

Amendment X

The powers not delegated to the United States by the Constitution, nor prohibited by it to the States, are reserved to the States respectively, or to the people.

= = =

"Liberty must at all hazards be supported. We have a right to it, derived from our Maker. But if we had not, our fathers have earned it for us, at the expense of their ease, their estates, their pleasure, and their blood." – John Adams (1735-1826), a U.S. Founding Father; First U.S. Vice President; Second U.S. President

"A Bill of Rights is what the people are entitled to against every government, and what no just government should refuse, or rest on inference." – Thomas Jefferson (1743-1826), a U.S. Founding Father; principal author of the Declaration of Independence; 3rd U.S. President

"The Bill of Rights wasn't enacted to give us any rights. It was enacted so the Government could not take away from us any rights that we already had." – Kenneth Eade (1957-   ), an American environmental and political activist; author

"The Framers of the Bill of Rights did not purport to "create" rights. Rather, they designed the Bill of Rights to prohibit our Government from infringing rights and liberties presumed to be preexisting."
– William J. Brennan, Jr. (1906-1997), an Associate Justice of U.S. Supreme Court from 1956-1990

"Can any of you seriously say the Bill of Rights could get through Congress today? It wouldn't even get out of committee."
– F. Lee Bailey (1933-   ), an American former criminal defense attorney

Our U.S. "Pledge of Allegiance"

Official versions (*changes in **bold underline***)
1892 (first version)
"I pledge allegiance to my Flag and the republic for which it stands, one nation indivisible, with liberty and justice for all."
1892 to 1922
"I pledge allegiance to my Flag and **to** the republic for which it stands: one nation indivisible, with liberty and justice for all."
1923
"I pledge allegiance to **the** Flag **of the United States** and to the republic for which it stands; one Nation indivisible with liberty and justice for all."
1924 to 1954
"I pledge allegiance to the Flag of the United States **of America,** and to the republic for which it stands; one Nation indivisible with liberty and justice for all."
1954 (current version)
"I pledge allegiance to the Flag of the United States of America, and to the Republic for which it stands, one Nation **under God,** indivisible, with liberty and justice for all."

Section 4 of the U.S. Flag Code states in part that The Pledge of Allegiance to the Flag should ". . . be rendered by standing at attention facing the flag with the right hand over the heart. When not in uniform men should remove any non-religious headdress with their right hand and hold it at the left shoulder, the hand being over the heart. Persons in uniform should remain silent, face the flag, and render the military salute."

<u>A Brief History of our "Pledge of Allegiance"</u>

As shown on the previous page, the "original" **Pledge of Allegiance** read *"I pledge allegiance to my Flag and the Republic for which it stands- one nation indivisible- with liberty and justice for all."* Words written by Francis Bellamy, for Boston, Massachusetts based magazine, *The Youth's Companion,* and published on September 8, 1892, to provide students something special to repeat on Columbus Day that year. After reprinted on circulars distributed to schools throughout the country, on October 12, 1892, millions of school children repeated this *Pledge of Allegiance,* thereby starting a nation-wide school-day practice. Thereafter, on June 14, 1923, at the first National Flag Conference in Washington D.C., the words "my flag" were replaced with the formally-adopted words "the Flag of the United States." Finally, in 1942, the *Pledge of Allegiance* was officially recognized by our U.S. Congress. Then, in June 1943, the Supreme Court ruled that, as protected by the free-speech clause of the First Amendment to our U.S. Constitution, school children could not be forced to salute the Flag or say the Pledge, nor be punished for not doing so. Years later, in June 1954, the words "under God" were added by an amendment. At that time, President Dwight D. Eisenhower reportedly expressed, *"In this way we are reaffirming the transcendence of religious faith in America's heritage and future; in this way we shall constantly strengthen those spiritual weapons which forever will be our country's most powerful resource in peace and war."*

= = =

And, in our "politically-correctness-gone-mad" world of today, even "suggesting" that our children participate in such patriotic acts as saluting our U.S. Flag or reciting the Pledge of Allegiance, can often result in lawsuits, recrimination, someone being "offended," as well as teachers being suspended or fired! Clearly, our country is in much need of an appropriate measure of **"patriotic-correctness"** to ensure an at least **equal-balance** with the liberty-threatening **"political-correctness"** agenda being imposed upon us.

Our U.S. National Anthem
The Star Spangled Banner
(September 20, 1814 — By Francis Scott Key)

O say can you see, by the dawn's early light,
What so proudly we hail'd at the twilight's last gleaming,
Whose broad stripes and bright stars through the perilous fight
O'er the ramparts we watch'd were so gallantly streaming?
And the rocket's red glare, the bombs bursting in air,
Gave proof through the night that our flag was still there,
O say does that star-spangled banner yet wave
O'er the land of the free and the home of the brave?

On the shore dimly seen through the mists of the deep
Where the foe's haughty host in dread silence reposes,
What is that which the breeze, o'er the towering steep,
As it fitfully blows, half conceals, half discloses?
Now it catches the gleam of the morning's first beam,
In full glory reflected now shines in the stream,
'Tis the star-spangled banner - O long may it wave
O'er the land of the free and the home of the brave!

And where is that band who so vauntingly swore,
That the havoc of war and the battle's confusion
A home and a Country should leave us no more?
Their blood has wash'd out their foul footstep's pollution.
No refuge could save the hireling and slave
From the terror of flight or the gloom of the grave,
And the star-spangled banner in triumph doth wave
O'er the land of the free and the home of the brave.

O thus be it ever when freemen shall stand
Between their lov'd home and the war's desolation!
Blest with vict'ry and peace may the heav'n rescued land
Praise the power that hath made and preserv'd us a nation!
Then conquer we must, when our cause it is just,
And this be our motto - "In God is our trust,"
And the star-spangled banner in triumph shall wave
O'er the land of the free and the home of the brave.

A Brief History of Our U.S. National Anthem
"The Star-Spangled Banner"

The lyrics to "The Star-Spangled Banner" were composed by Francis Scott Key, an American lawyer, on September 14, 1814. After he witnessed the massive overnight British bombardment of Fort McHenry in Maryland during the War of 1812. Key watched the siege while being detained on a British ship, and penned our country's famous anthem after seeing in awe that the Fort McHenry flag had survived the awesome British assault of reportedly 1,800 bombs.

After being circulated as a handbill, the lyrics were eventually published in a Baltimore newspaper on September 20, 1814, and later set to the tune of "To Anacreon in Heaven," a popular English song.

Throughout the 19th century, "The Star-Spangled Banner" was considered the national anthem by most branches of our U.S. armed forces and other groups. However, it was not until 1916, and President Woodrow Wilson's signing of an executive order, that it was officially designated as such. Then, in March 1931, Congress passed an act confirming President Wilson's presidential order, soon followed by President Hoover signing it into law on March 3, 1931.

An "Eight-Page" Listing of 438 Federal Government Agencies!

While falsely preaching "simplicity" and "efficiency" of operations, our Federal Government continues to grow its "agencies" under a broad mix of terms and titles, such as: Agencies, Bureaus, Commissions, Departments, Services, Offices, Boards, Corporations, Foundations, Administrations, Councils, Divisions, etc., etc. A practice especially helpful in making it difficult, if not impossible, to track ultimate responsibility; accountability; and outdated or duplicated functions, etc. Being of course among the primary aims.

= = =

- Administration Office, Executive Office of the President
  - o National Commission on Fiscal Responsibility and Reform
- Administrative Conference of the United States
- Administrative Office of United States Courts
- Advocacy and Outreach Office
- African Development Foundation
- Agency for Healthcare Research and Quality
- Agency for International Development
  - o International Development Cooperation Agency
- Agency for Toxic Substances and Disease Registry
- Aging Administration
- Agricultural Marketing Service
- Agricultural Research Service
- Agriculture Department
  - o Advocacy and Outreach Office
  - o Agricultural Marketing Service
  - o Agricultural Research Service
  - o Animal and Plant Health Inspection Service
  - o Commodity Credit Corporation
  - o Cooperative State Research, Education, and Extension Service
  - o Economic Analysis Staff
  - o Economic Research Service
  - o Energy Policy and New Uses Office
  - o Farm Service Agency
  - o Federal Crop Insurance Corporation
  - o Food and Consumer Service
  - o Food and Nutrition Service
  - o Food Safety and Inspection Service
  - o Foreign Agricultural Service
  - o Forest Service
  - o Grain Inspection, Packers and Stockyards Administration
  - o Inspector General Office, Agriculture Department
  - o National Agricultural Library
  - o National Agricultural Statistics Service
  - o National Institute of Food and Agriculture
  - o Natural Resources Conservation Service
  - o Operations Office
  - o Procurement and Property Management, Office of
  - o Risk Management Agency
  - o Rural Business-Cooperative Service
  - o Rural Housing and Community Development Service
  - o Rural Housing Service
  - o Rural Telephone Bank
  - o Rural Utilities Service
  - o Transportation Office
- Air Force Department
- Air Quality National Commission
- Air Transportation Stabilization Board

- Alaska Power Administration
- Alcohol and Tobacco Tax and Trade Bureau
- Alcohol, Tobacco, Firearms, and Explosives Bureau
- American Battle Monuments Commission
- Amtrak Reform Council
- Animal and Plant Health Inspection Service
- Antitrust Division
- Antitrust Modernization Commission
- Appalachian Regional Commission
- Appalachian States Low-Level Radioactive Waste Commission
- Architect of the Capitol
- Architectural and Transportation Barriers Compliance Board
- Arctic Research Commission
- Armed Forces Retirement Home
- Arms Control and Disarmament Agency
- Army Department
- Assassination Records Review Board
- Barry M. Goldwater Scholarship and Excellence in Education Foundation
- Bipartisan Commission on Entitlement and Tax Reform
- Board of Directors of the Hope for Homeowners Program
- Bonneville Power Administration
- Broadcasting Board of Governors
- Bureau of the Fiscal Service
- Census Bureau
- Census Monitoring Board
- Centers for Disease Control and Prevention
- Centers for Medicare & Medicaid Services
- Central Intelligence Agency
- Chemical Safety and Hazard Investigation Board
- Child Support Enforcement Office
- Children and Families Administration
- Christopher Columbus Quincentenary Jubilee Commission
- Civil Rights Commission
- Coast Guard
- Commerce Department
  - o Census Bureau
  - o Economic Analysis Bureau
  - o Economic Development Administration
  - o Economics and Statistics Administration
  - o Export Administration Bureau
  - o Foreign-Trade Zones Board
  - o Industry and Security Bureau
  - o International Trade Administration
  - o Minority Business Development Agency
  - o National Institute of Standards and Technology
  - o National Oceanic and Atmospheric Administration
  - o National Shipping Authority
  - o National Technical Information Service
  - o National Telecommunications and Information Administration
  - o Patent and Trademark Office
  - o Technology Administration
  - o Travel and Tourism Administration
- Commercial Space Transportation Office
- Commission of Fine Arts
- Commission on Immigration Reform
- Commission on Protecting and Reducing Government Secrecy
- Commission on Review of Overseas Military Facility Structure of the United States
- Commission on Structural Alternatives for the Federal Courts of Appeals
- Commission on the Advancement of Federal Law Enforcement
- Commission on the Bicentennial of the United States Constitution
- Commission on the Future of the United States Aerospace Industry
- Commission on the Social Security Notch Issue
- Committee for Purchase From People Who Are Blind or Severely Disabled
- Committee for the Implementation of Textile Agreements
- Commodity Credit Corporation
- Commodity Futures Trading Commission
- Community Development Financial Institutions Fund
- Community Living Administration
- Competitiveness Policy Council
- Comptroller of the Currency
- Congressional Budget Office
- Consumer Financial Protection Bureau
- Consumer Product Safety Commission
- Cooperative State Research, Education, and Extension Service
- Coordinating Council on Juvenile Justice and Delinquency Prevention
- Copyright Office, Library of Congress

- Copyright Royalty Board
- Copyright Royalty Judges, Library of Congress
- Corporation for National and Community Service
- Council of the Inspectors General on Integrity and Efficiency
- Council on Environmental Quality
- Counsel to the President
- Court Services and Offender Supervision Agency for the District of Columbia
- Crime and Security in U.S. Seaports, Interagency Commission
- Customs Service

- Defense Acquisition Regulations System
- Defense Base Closure and Realignment Commission
- Defense Contract Audit Agency
- Defense Criminal Investigative Service
- Defense Department
  - Air Force Department
  - Army Department
  - Defense Acquisition Regulations System
  - Defense Contract Audit Agency
  - Defense Criminal Investigative Service
  - Defense Information Systems Agency
  - Defense Intelligence Agency
  - Defense Investigative Service
  - Defense Logistics Agency
  - Defense Mapping Agency
  - Defense Special Weapons Agency
  - Engineers Corps
  - National Geospatial-Intelligence Agency
  - National Security Agency/Central Security Service
  - Navy Department
  - Uniformed Services University of the Health Sciences
- Defense Information Systems Agency
- Defense Intelligence Agency
- Defense Investigative Service
- Defense Logistics Agency
- Defense Mapping Agency
- Defense Nuclear Facilities Safety Board
- Defense Special Weapons Agency
- Delaware River Basin Commission
- Denali Commission
- Disability Employment Policy Office
- Drug Enforcement Administration
- Economic Analysis Bureau
- Economic Analysis Staff
- Economic Development Administration
- Economic Research Service
- Economics and Statistics Administration
- Education Department
- Election Assistance Commission
- Electronic Commerce Advisory Commission
- Emergency Oil and Gas Guaranteed Loan Board
- Emergency Steel Guarantee Loan Board
- Employee Benefits Security Administration
- Employees Compensation Appeals Board
- Employment and Training Administration
- Employment Standards Administration
- Energy Department
  - Alaska Power Administration
  - Bonneville Power Administration
  - Energy Efficiency and Renewable Energy Office
  - Energy Information Administration
  - Energy Research Office
  - Environment Office, Energy Department
  - Federal Energy Regulatory Commission
  - Hearings and Appeals Office, Energy Department
  - Minority Economic Impact Office
  - National Nuclear Security Administration
  - Nuclear Energy Office
  - Southeastern Power Administration
  - Southwestern Power Administration
  - Western Area Power Administration
- Energy Efficiency and Renewable Energy Office
- Energy Information Administration
- Energy Policy and New Uses Office
- Energy Research Office
- Engineers Corps
- Engraving and Printing Bureau
- Environment Office, Energy Department
- Environmental Protection Agency
- Equal Employment Opportunity Commission
- Executive Council on Integrity and Efficiency
- Executive Office for Immigration Review
- Executive Office of the President
  - Administration Office, Executive Office of the President
  - Council on Environmental Quality
  - Counsel to the President
- Export Administration Bureau
- Export-Import Bank
- Family Assistance Office
- Farm Credit Administration
- Farm Credit System Insurance Corporation
- Farm Service Agency
- Federal Accounting Standards Advisory Board
- Federal Acquisition Regulation System
- Federal Aviation Administration
- Federal Bureau of Investigation

- Federal Communications Commission
- Federal Contract Compliance Programs Office
- Federal Crop Insurance Corporation
- Federal Deposit Insurance Corporation
- Federal Election Commission
- Federal Emergency Management Agency
- Federal Energy Regulatory Commission
- Federal Financial Institutions Examination Council
- Federal Highway Administration
- Federal Housing Enterprise Oversight Office
- Federal Housing Finance Agency
- Federal Housing Finance Board
- Federal Labor Relations Authority
    - o Federal Service Impasses Panel
- Federal Law Enforcement Training Center
- Federal Maritime Commission
- Federal Mediation and Conciliation Service
- Federal Mine Safety and Health Review Commission
- Federal Motor Carrier Safety Administration
- Federal Pay, Advisory Committee
- Federal Prison Industries
- Federal Procurement Policy Office
- Federal Railroad Administration
- Federal Register Office
- Federal Register, Administrative Committee
- Federal Reserve System
- Federal Retirement Thrift Investment Board
- Federal Service Impasses Panel
- Federal Trade Commission
- Federal Transit Administration
- Financial Crimes Enforcement Network
- Financial Crisis Inquiry Commission
- Financial Research Office
- Financial Stability Oversight Council
- First Responder Network Authority
- Fiscal Service
- Fish and Wildlife Service
- Food and Consumer Service
- Food and Drug Administration
- Food and Nutrition Service
- Food Safety and Inspection Service
- Foreign Agricultural Service
- Foreign Assets Control Office
- Foreign Claims Settlement Commission
- Foreign Service Grievance Board
- Foreign Service Impasse Disputes Panel
- Foreign Service Labor Relations Board
- Foreign-Trade Zones Board
- Forest Service
- General Services Administration
- Geographic Names Board
- Geological Survey
- Government Accountability Office
- Government Ethics Office
- Government National Mortgage Association
- Government Publishing Office
- Grain Inspection, Packers and Stockyards Administration
- Gulf Coast Ecosystem Restoration Council
- Harry S. Truman Scholarship Foundation
- Health and Human Services Department
    - o Agency for Healthcare Research and Quality
    - o Agency for Toxic Substances and Disease Registry
    - o Aging Administration
    - o Centers for Disease Control and Prevention
    - o Centers for Medicare & Medicaid Services
    - o Child Support Enforcement Office
    - o Children and Families Administration
    - o Community Living Administration
    - o Family Assistance Office
    - o Food and Drug Administration
    - o Health Care Finance Administration
    - o Health Resources and Services Administration
    - o Indian Health Service
    - o Inspector General Office, Health and Human Services Department
    - o National Institutes of Health
    - o National Library of Medicine
    - o Program Support Center
    - o Public Health Service
    - o Refugee Resettlement Office
    - o Substance Abuse and Mental Health Services Administration
- Health Care Finance Administration
- Health Resources and Services Administration
- Hearings and Appeals Office, Energy Department
- Hearings and Appeals Office, Interior Department
- Historic Preservation, Advisory Council
- Homeland Security Department

- o Coast Guard
- o Federal Emergency Management Agency
- o Federal Law Enforcement Training Center
- o National Communications System
- o Secret Service
- o Transportation Security Administration
- o U.S. Citizenship and Immigration Services
- o U.S. Customs and Border Protection
- o U.S. Immigration and Customs Enforcement
- Housing and Urban Development Department
- o Federal Housing Enterprise Oversight Office
- o Government National Mortgage Association
- Immigration and Naturalization Service
- Indian Affairs Bureau
- Indian Arts and Crafts Board
- Indian Health Service
- Indian Trust Transition Office
- Industry and Security Bureau
- Information Security Oversight Office
- Inspector General Office, Agriculture Department
- Inspector General Office, Health and Human Services Department
- Institute of American Indian and Alaska Native Culture and Arts Development
- Institute of Museum and Library Services
- Inter-American Foundation
- Interagency Floodplain Management Review Committee
- Intergovernmental Relations Advisory Commission
- Interior Department
- o Fish and Wildlife Service
- o Geological Survey
- o Hearings and Appeals Office, Interior Department
- o Indian Affairs Bureau
- o Indian Trust Transition Office
- o Land Management Bureau
- o Minerals Management Service
- o Mines Bureau
- o National Biological Service
- o National Civilian Community Corps
- o National Indian Gaming Commission
- o National Park Service
- o Natural Resources Revenue Office
- o Ocean Energy Management Bureau
- o Ocean Energy Management, Regulation, and Enforcement Bureau
- o Reclamation Bureau
- o Safety and Environmental Enforcement Bureau
- o Special Trustee for American Indians Office
- o Surface Mining Reclamation and Enforcement Office
- Internal Revenue Service
- International Boundary and Water Commission, United States and Mexico
- International Broadcasting Board
- International Development Cooperation Agency
- International Investment Office
- International Joint Commission-United States and Canada
- International Organizations Employees Loyalty Board
- International Trade Administration
- International Trade Commission
- Interstate Commerce Commission
- James Madison Memorial Fellowship Foundation
- Japan-United States Friendship Commission
- Joint Board for Enrollment of Actuaries
- Judicial Conference of the United States
- Judicial Review Commission on Foreign Asset Control
- Justice Department
- o Alcohol, Tobacco, Firearms, and Explosives Bureau
- o Antitrust Division
- o Drug Enforcement Administration
- o Executive Office for Immigration Review
- o Federal Bureau of Investigation
- o Federal Prison Industries
- o Foreign Claims Settlement Commission
- o Immigration and Naturalization Service
- o Justice Programs Office
- o Juvenile Justice and Delinquency Prevention Office
- o National Institute of Corrections
- o National Institute of Justice
- o Parole Commission
- o Prisons Bureau
- o United States Marshals Service
- Justice Programs Office
- o Victims of Crime Office
- Juvenile Justice and Delinquency Prevention Office
- Labor Department
- o Disability Employment Policy Office
- o Employee Benefits Security Administration
- o Employees Compensation Appeals Board
- o Employment and Training Administration
- o Employment Standards Administration

    o   Federal Contract Compliance Programs Office
    o   Labor Statistics Bureau
    o   Labor-Management Standards Office
    o   Mine Safety and Health Administration
    o   Occupational Safety and Health Administration
    o   Pension and Welfare Benefits Administration
    o   Veterans Employment and Training Service
    o   Wage and Hour Division
    o   Workers Compensation Programs Office
 •   Labor Statistics Bureau
 •   Labor-Management Standards Office
 •   Land Management Bureau
 •   Legal Services Corporation
 •   Library of Congress
    o   Copyright Office, Library of Congress
    o   Copyright Royalty Board
 •   Local Television Loan Guarantee Board
 •   Management and Budget Office
    o   Federal Procurement Policy Office
 •   Marine Mammal Commission
 •   Maritime Administration
 •   Medicare Payment Advisory Commission
 •   Merit Systems Protection Board
 •   Military Compensation and Retirement Modernization Commission
 •   Millennium Challenge Corporation
 •   Mine Safety and Health Administration
 •   Minerals Management Service
 •   Mines Bureau
 •   Minority Business Development Agency
 •   Minority Economic Impact Office
 •   Mississippi River Commission
 •   Monetary Offices
 •   Morris K. Udall and Stewart L. Udall Foundation
 •   National Aeronautics and Space Administration
 •   National Agricultural Library
 •   National Agricultural Statistics Service
 •   National Archives and Records Administration
    o   Federal Register Office
    o   Information Security Oversight Office
    o   National Historical Publications and Records Commission
 •   National Bankruptcy Review Commission
 •   National Biological Service
 •   National Bipartisan Commission on Future of Medicare
 •   National Capital Planning Commission
 •   National Civilian Community Corps
 •   National Commission on Fiscal Responsibility and Reform
 •   National Commission on Intermodal Transportation
 •   National Commission on Libraries and Information Science
 •   National Commission on Manufactured Housing
 •   National Commission on Terrorist Attacks Upon the United States
 •   National Commission on the Cost of Higher Education
 •   National Communications System
 •   National Consumer Cooperative Bank
 •   National Council on Disability
 •   National Counterintelligence Center
 •   National Credit Union Administration
 •   National Crime Prevention and Privacy Compact Council
 •   National Economic Council
 •   National Education Goals Panel
 •   National Endowment for the Arts
 •   National Endowment for the Humanities
 •   National Foundation on the Arts and the Humanities
    o   Institute of Museum and Library Services
    o   National Endowment for the Arts
    o   National Endowment for the Humanities
 •   National Gambling Impact Study Commission
 •   National Geospatial-Intelligence Agency
 •   National Highway Traffic Safety Administration
 •   National Historical Publications and Records Commission
 •   National Indian Gaming Commission
 •   National Institute for Literacy
 •   National Institute of Corrections
 •   National Institute of Food and Agriculture
 •   National Institute of Justice
 •   National Institute of Standards and Technology
 •   National Institutes of Health
 •   National Intelligence, Office of the National Director
 •   National Labor Relations Board
 •   National Library of Medicine
 •   National Mediation Board
 •   National Nanotechnology Coordination Office
 •   National Nuclear Security Administration
 •   National Oceanic and Atmospheric Administration
 •   National Park Service
 •   National Partnership for Reinventing Government
 •   National Prison Rape Elimination Commission

- National Railroad Passenger Corporation
- National Science Foundation
- National Security Agency/Central Security Service
- National Security Council
- National Shipping Authority
- National Skill Standards Board
- National Technical Information Service
- National Telecommunications and Information Administration
  - o First Responder Network Authority
- National Transportation Safety Board
- National Women's Business Council
- Natural Resources Conservation Service
- Natural Resources Revenue Office
- Navajo and Hopi Indian Relocation Office
- Navy Department
- Neighborhood Reinvestment Corporation
- Northeast Dairy Compact Commission
- Northeast Interstate Low-Level Radioactive Waste Commission
- Nuclear Energy Office
- Nuclear Regulatory Commission
- Nuclear Waste Technical Review Board
- Occupational Safety and Health Administration
- Occupational Safety and Health Review Commission
- Ocean Energy Management Bureau
- Ocean Energy Management, Regulation, and Enforcement Bureau
- Ocean Policy Commission
- Office of Motor Carrier Safety
- Office of National Drug Control Policy
- Office of Policy Development
- Oklahoma City National Memorial Trust
- Operations Office
- Ounce of Prevention Council
- Overseas Private Investment Corporation
- Pacific Northwest Electric Power and Conservation Planning Council
- Panama Canal Commission
- Parole Commission
- Patent and Trademark Office
- Peace Corps
- Pension and Welfare Benefits Administration
- Pension Benefit Guaranty Corporation
- Personnel Management Office
- Physician Payment Review Commission
- Pipeline and Hazardous Materials Safety Administration
- Postal Rate Commission
- Postal Regulatory Commission
- Postal Service
- President's Council on Integrity and Efficiency
- President's Council on Sustainable Development
- President's Critical Infrastructure Protection Board
- President's Economic Policy Advisory Board
- Presidential Advisory Committee on Gulf War Veterans' Illnesses
- Presidential Commission on Assignment of Women in the Armed Forces
- Presidential Documents
- Presidio Trust
- Prisons Bureau
- Privacy and Civil Liberties Oversight Board
- Procurement and Property Management, Office of
- Program Support Center
- Prospective Payment Assessment Commission
- Public Debt Bureau
- Public Health Service
- Railroad Retirement Board
- Reagan-Udall Foundation for the Food and Drug Administration
- Reclamation Bureau
- Recovery Accountability and Transparency Board
- Refugee Resettlement Office
- Regulatory Information Service Center
- Research and Innovative Technology Administration
- Research and Special Programs Administration
- Resolution Trust Corporation
- Risk Management Agency
- Rural Business-Cooperative Service
- Rural Housing and Community Development Service
- Rural Housing Service
- Rural Telephone Bank
- Rural Utilities Service
- Safety and Environmental Enforcement Bureau
- Saint Lawrence Seaway Development Corporation
- Science and Technology Policy Office
- Secret Service
- Securities and Exchange Commission
- Selective Service System
- Small Business Administration
- Smithsonian Institution
- Social Security Administration
- Southeastern Power Administration

- Southwestern Power Administration
- Special Counsel Office
- Special Inspector General for Afghanistan Reconstruction
- Special Inspector General For Iraq Reconstruction
- Special Trustee for American Indians Office
- State Department
- State Justice Institute
- Substance Abuse and Mental Health Services Administration
- Surface Mining Reclamation and Enforcement Office
- Surface Transportation Board
- Susquehanna River Basin Commission
- Technology Administration
- Tennessee Valley Authority
- The White House Office
- Thrift Depositor Protection Oversight Board
- Thrift Supervision Office
- Trade and Development Agency
- Trade Representative, Office of United States
- Transportation Department
  - Commercial Space Transportation Office
  - Federal Aviation Administration
  - Federal Highway Administration
  - Federal Motor Carrier Safety Administration
  - Federal Railroad Administration
  - Federal Transit Administration
  - Maritime Administration
  - National Highway Traffic Safety Administration
  - Office of Motor Carrier Safety
  - Pipeline and Hazardous Materials Safety Administration
  - Research and Innovative Technology Administration
  - Research and Special Programs Administration
  - Saint Lawrence Seaway Development Corporation
  - Surface Transportation Board
  - Transportation Statistics Bureau
- Transportation Office
- Transportation Security Administration
- Transportation Statistics Bureau
- Travel and Tourism Administration
- Treasury Department
  - Alcohol and Tobacco Tax and Trade Bureau
  - Bureau of the Fiscal Service
  - Community Development Financial Institutions Fund
  - Comptroller of the Currency
  - Customs Service
  - Engraving and Printing Bureau
  - Financial Crimes Enforcement Network
  - Financial Research Office
  - Fiscal Service
  - Foreign Assets Control Office
  - Internal Revenue Service
  - International Investment Office
  - Monetary Offices
  - Public Debt Bureau
  - Thrift Supervision Office
  - United States Mint
- Twenty-First Century Workforce Commission
- U.S. Citizenship and Immigration Services
- U.S. Customs and Border Protection
- U.S. House of Representatives
- U.S. Immigration and Customs Enforcement
- U.S. Trade Deficit Review Commission
- U.S.-China Economic and Security Review Commission
- Uniformed Services University of the Health Sciences
- United States Enrichment Corporation
- United States Information Agency
- United States Institute of Peace
- United States Marshals Service
- United States Mint
- United States Sentencing Commission
- Utah Reclamation Mitigation and Conservation Commission
- Valles Caldera Trust
- Veterans Affairs Department
- Veterans Employment and Training Service
- Victims of Crime Office
- Wage and Hour Division
- Western Area Power Administration
- Women's Business Enterprise Interagency Committee
- Women's Progress Commemoration Commission
- Workers Compensation Programs Office

"As government expands, liberty contracts."

— Ronald Reagan (1911-2004), 40th U.S. President

Terms & Definitions

"Agency Debt" (Federal Government): So-called "Agency Debt" is the amount of debt outstanding issued by Federal Agencies, such as, the Federal Home Loan Bank (FHLB) and the "Ginnie Mae"– Government National Mortgage Association (GNMA), as well as government-sponsored enterprises, such as Fannie Mae and Freddie Mac. Historically, Agency Debt has not been included in the total debt of the United States government as published by the U.S. Department of the Treasury.

Budget: An estimate of income and spending for a set period of time.

Budget (Federal Government): The federal government's estimate of spending and revenue (income) for each Fiscal Year. Most of the revenue comes from taxes. Such as, taxes on family incomes, business profits, and imports (custom duties and tariffs). As well as taxes on activities the government wants to discourage, such as, cigarette smoking and alcohol use. In addition, there are taxes on activities, such as on gasoline, to pay for related activities, such as building roads.

Budget Deficit: A budget deficit occurs when an individual, business, or government, budgets more spending than there is income (revenue) available to pay for the spending, over a specific period of time. Debt is the total amount of deficits accumulated over time.

Bureaucracy: A system of government in which most of the important decisions are made by state officials rather than by elected representatives.

Congressional Budget Office (CBO): A federal agency within the legislative branch of the U.S. Government that provides budget and economic information to the U.S. Congress.

Debt: Something, typically money, that is owed or due.

Debt Crisis (re: a country's economy): When a country's debt continues indefinitely to grow faster than the country's economy.

Debt-to-GDP Ratio: In economics, the debt-to-GDP ratio is the ratio between a country's government debt and its gross domestic product (GDP) measured in years. A low debt-to-GDP ratio indicates an economy that produces and sells enough goods and services to pay back debts without taking on additional debt.

Deficit: The amount by which something, especially a sum of money, is too small. An excess of spending or liabilities over income or assets in a given period of time.

<u>Deficit Spending (by government)</u>: Government spending, in excess of income (revenues), of funds raised by borrowing or printing additional money, rather than from taxation.

<u>Deflation (Economic)</u>: A decrease in the general price level of goods and services. Deflation occurs when the inflation rate falls below 0% (a negative inflation rate). Inflation reduces the value of money over time, but deflation increases it. This allows one to buy more goods and services than before with the same amount of currency. Economists generally believe that deflation is a problem in a modern economy because it increases the real value of debt, especially if the deflation is unexpected. Deflation may also aggravate recessions and lead to a deflationary spiral.

<u>Depression (economic)</u>: A long and severe recession in an economy or market.

<u>Federal Home Loan Bank (FHLB)</u>: A federal government agency is an organization created by the Federal Home Loan Bank Act of 1932 to increase the amount of funds available for lending institutions who provide mortgages and similar loan agreements to individuals.

<u>Federal Reserve</u>: The Federal Reserve's mandate is to maintain price stability and low unemployment. It prints money based on the assumption that increasing money supply will boost jobs. Towards these ends, the Federal Reserve writes blank checks to itself from an unlimited checking account. Then through various financial mechanisms, buys US debt (government bonds) with newly "printed" Federal Reserve Notes (money). Through this process, new money is introduced into the financial system.

Fiscal: Relating to government revenue (income), especially taxes.

Fiscal Year: The federal government's **fiscal year** is the accounting period which begins on October 1 and ends on September 30. The **fiscal year** is designated by the **calendar year** in which it ends; for example, **fiscal year 2017** began on October 1, 2016 and ended on September 30, 2017.

"Ginnie Mae" – Government National Mortgage Association (GNMA): A federal government agency that aims to expand affordable housing in America by insuring liquidity for government-insured mortgages, including those insured by the Federal Housing Administration (FHA), the Veterans Administration (VA) and the Rural Housing Administration (RHA).

Gross Domestic Product (GDP) [Purchasing Power Parity]: This entry gives the gross domestic product (GDP) or value of all final goods and services produced within a nation in a given year. A nation's GDP at purchasing power parity (PPP) exchange rates is the sum value of all goods and services produced in the country valued at prices prevailing in the United States in the year noted.

<u>Gross National Product (GNP)</u>: The value of all final goods and services produced within a nation in a given year, plus income earned by its citizens abroad, minus income earned by foreigners from domestic production.

<u>Inflation (economic)</u>: A general increase in prices and fall in the purchasing value of money. Economists generally believe that high rates of inflation are caused by an excessive growth of the money supply.

<u>Interest</u>: Money paid regularly at a particular rate for the use of money lent, or for delaying the repayment of a debt.

<u>Interest Rate</u>: The proportion of a loan that is charged as interest to the borrower, typically expressed as an annual percentage of the loan outstanding.

<u>Liberty</u>: The state of being free within society from oppressive restrictions imposed by authority on one's way of life, behavior, or political views. The freedom to pursue one's own interests and preferences.

<u>Money (Economics)</u>: Something serving as a "medium of exchange"; a unit of accounting; a store of value. For example, the U.S. Dollar is a medium of exchange since we all agree to accept it in making transactions (buying and selling).

Office of Management and Budget (OMB): The business division of the Executive Office of the President of the U.S. that administers the U.S. Federal Budget and oversees the performance of Federal Agencies.

Recession (economic): A period of temporary economic decline during which trade and industry activity are reduced; generally identified by a fall in gross domestic product (GDP) in two successive quarters.

Social Security Trust Funds: The Social Security trust funds are financial accounts in the U.S. Treasury. There are two separate Social Security trust funds. The Old-Age and Survivors Insurance (OASI) Trust Fund pays retirement and survivors benefits, and the Disability Insurance (DI) Trust Fund pays disability benefits.

"Tipping Point" (re: Country's Economy): The point where a country risks spiraling into a vicious cycle of higher interest rates that put pressure on budgeting; making debt riskier and causing interest rates to rise even higher; ultimately leading to economic crisis.

Unfunded Liability: The amount, at any given time, by which future payment obligations exceed the present and forecasted value of the funds available to pay those obligations. For example, unsustainable promises regarding future Social Security, Medicare, Federal Employee, and Veterans benefits, etc.

<u>U.S. Department of The Treasury (USDT)</u>: An executive department and the treasury of the U.S. Federal Government. Established by an Act of Congress in 1789 to manage government revenue. The Treasury prints all paper currency and mints all coins in circulation through the Bureau of Engraving and Printing and the U.S. Mint, respectively; collects all federal taxes through the Internal Revenue Service; manages U.S. government debt instruments; licenses and supervises banks and thrift institutions; and advises the legislative and executive branches on matters of fiscal policy.

<u>U.S. National Debt</u>: Debt managed by the U.S. Treasury Department through its Bureau of the Public Debt, and made up of the combination of the following two broad categories:

(1.) *Public Debt*: This is money our federal government borrows from American investors; foreign investors; foreign governments; etc., through the sale of U.S. Treasury Bills, Notes, and Bonds; U.S. Savings Bonds; etc.

(2.) *Intra-governmental Debt:* This is money our federal government owes itself. Such as money borrowed from the Social Security and Medicare trust funds; Military Retirement funds; Civil Service funds; Federal Reserve Banks; etc.

"As a very important source of strength and security, cherish public credit. One method of preserving it is, to use it as sparingly as possible; avoiding occasions of expense by cultivating peace, but remembering also that timely disbursements to prepare for danger frequently prevent much greater disbursements to repel it; avoiding likewise the accumulation of debt, not only by shunning occasions of expense, but by vigorous exertions in time of peace to discharge the debts, which unavoidable wars may have occasioned, not ungenerously throwing upon posterity the burden, which we ourselves ought to bear." – George Washington (1732-1799), a U.S. Founding Father, first U.S. President, 1789-1797. [Words from his Farewell Address, September 17, 1796]

References & Recommended Reading

(Listed Alphabetically by Author's Last Name)

Book Title	Author
The Torah; Holy Bible; Qur'an (Koran); and/or Other Religious Text of one's respective Faith or otherwise interest. *[Listed in chronological order.]*	(Most literal translation and reader-friendly format of choice.)
Crisis Of Character	Gary J. Byrne
The Debt Bomb	Senator Tom Coburn & John Hart
There Goes My Social Life: From Clueless to Conservative	Stacey Dash
Hillary's America	Dinesh D'Souza
Clinton Cash	Chuck Dixon; Brett R. Smith; Peter Schweizer
All I Really Need To Know I Learned In Kindergarten	Robert Fulghum
<ul><li>Because They Hate</li><li>They Must Be Stopped: Why We Must Defeat Radical Islam and How We Can Do It</li></ul>	Brigitte Gabriel
The Haldeman Diaries – Inside The Nixon White House	H. R. Haldeman (Introduction and Afterword by Stephen E. Ambrose)
The Federalist Papers	Alexander Hamilton, James Madison, & John Jay (Introduction by Gary Wills)
See Something, Say Nothing: A Homeland Security Officer Exposes the Government's Submission to Jihad	Philip Haney & Art Moore

References & Recommended Reading – *(Continued)*
(Listed Alphabetically by Author's Last Name)

Book Title	Author
Hostile Waters	Peter Huchthausen, Igor Kurdin, & R. Alan White
White House Burning	Simon Johnson James Kwak
Who Moved My Cheese?	Spencer Johnson
Two Incomes and Still Broke?	Linda Kelley
The Imitation Of Christ	Thomas A. Kempis
Lights Out	Ted Koppel
Trump Revealed	Michael Kranish; Mark Fisher
• The Liberty Amendments • Plunder and Deceit • Ameritopia • Liberty and Tyranny	Mark R. Levin
The Patriot's Reference	Edited by: Joel J. Miller & Kristen Parrish
Armageddon	Dick Morris; Eileen McGann
• Threats To Our Liberty & Survival • Killing "Life, Liberty, & Pursuit of Happiness • Destruction From Within • "Our" U.S. National Debt -- 101	William James Moore

References & Recommended Reading – *(Continued)*
(Listed Alphabetically by Author's Last Name)

Book Title	Author
• Killing Jesus • Killing Lincoln • Killing Patton • Killing Kennedy	Bill O'Reilly
I'm Not OK. You're Not OK. But It's OK!	Chris Padgett
Words That Inspired Him — A Lifetime Of Favorite Writings, Poems & Quotations	Norman Vincent Peal
The Most of Andy Rooney *(ESP Article: "Mr. Rooney goes to Washington")*	Andrew A. Rooney
• Liberalism Is A Mental Disorder • Stop The Coming Civil War • Countdown To Mecca • Government Zero • Scorched Earth • God, Faith, & Reason	Michael Savage
The Faith Explained	Leo J. Trese
• The Art of the Deal • Great Again	Donald J. Trump; Tony Schwartz Donald J. Trump
Enemies — A History of the FBI	Tim Weiner
• Mutterings Of An Old Man • I Felt The Floor Shake	Mike Womeldorff
• House Calls • Office Calls • Love Letters from a Marriage • Wisdom for a Woman • Wisdom for a Man	Gary Yarbrough, M.D.

References & Recommended Reading – *(Continued)*
(Random Listing)

Internet Link Title	Internet Address
U.S. National Debt Clock : Real Time	http://www.usdebtclock.org/
What Is National Debt?	https://www.thoughtco.com/definition-of-national-debt-1146136
The National Debt, Explained	http://theweek.com/articles/747998/national-debt-explained
How Big Is A Trillion Dollars In Singles? A Comparison	http://geekologie.com/2018/03/how-big-is-a-trillion-dollars-in-singles.php
United States GDP: 1960--2018	https://tradingeconomics.com/united-states/gdp
Treasury Direct: The Debt To The Penny And Who Holds It	https://www.treasurydirect.gov/NP/debt/current
Treasury Direct: Interest Expense On The Debt Outstanding	https://www.treasurydirect.gov/govt/reports/ir/ir_expense.htm
Office of Management and Budgeta: Budget and Spending	https://www.whitehouse.gov/issues/budget-spending/
Office of Management and Budget: Historical Tables	https://www.whitehouse.gov/omb/historical-tables/
Congressional Budget Office: Federal Debt and Interest Costs	https://www.cbo.gov/publication/21960
Central Intelligence Agency (CIA): The World Fact Book	https://www.cia.gov/library/publications/the-world-factbook/

References & Recommended Reading – *(Continued)*
(Random Listing)

Internet Link Title	Internet Address
U.S. Department of The Treasury	https://home.treasury.gov/
What Does one TRILLION Dollars Look Like? (Calculations & Dimensions)	http://www.pagetutor.com/trillion/calculations.html
U.S. Debt Visualized in $100 Bills	http://demonocracy.info/infographics/usa/us_debt/us_debt.html
Your Pension Is A Lie: There's $210 Trillion Of Liabilities Our Government Can't Fulfill	https://www.forbes.com/sites/johnmauldin/2017/10/10/your-pension-is-a-lie-theres-210-trillion-of-liabilities-our-government-cant-fulfill/#477483c265b1
Where Your Tax Dollars Go After You Pay The IRS	http://www.foxnews.com/politics/2018/04/23/where-your-tax-dollars-go-after-pay-irs.html
The Balance – What are Unfunded Liabilities?	https://www.thebalance.com/unfunded-liabilities-definition-and-examples 4159564
The Long Story of U.S. Debt, From 1780 to 2011, in 1 Little Chart	https://www.theatlantic.com/business/archive/2012/11/the-long-story-of-us-debt-from-1790-to-2011-in-1-little-chart/265185/
Debt Myths Debunked	https://www.usnews.com/opinion/economic-intelligence/articles/2016-12-01/myths-and-facts-about-the-us-federal-debt
At $21 Trillion, The National Debt Is Growing 36 Percent Faster Than The U.S. Economy	https://www.sovereignman.com/trends/at-21-trillion-the-national-debt-is-growing-36-faster-than-the-us-economy-23157/

References & Recommended Reading – *(Continued)*
(Random Listing)

Internet Link Title	Internet Address
WhiteHouse.gov The White	**https://www.whitehouse.gov/**
[PDF] Budget Of The U.S> Government – Whitehouse.gov	**https://www.whitehouse.gov/wp-content/uploads/2018/02/budget-fy2019.pdf**
U.S. Government Spending	**https://www.usgovernmentspending.com/**
Congressional Budget Office (CBO)	**https://www.cbo.gov/topics/budget**
The United States Social Security Administration	**https://www.ssa.gov/**
BS News Hour – Social Security Trust Fund Depleted in 17 Years	**https://www.pbs.org/newshour/economy/social-security-trust-fund-will-depleted-17-years-according-trustees-report**
FreedomWorks.org	**http://www.freedomworks.org/content/almost-62-percent-federal-spending-2018-baked-budgetary-cake**

"Enjoy the Little Things"

"Enjoy the little things, for one day you may look back and realize they were the big things." — Robert Brault

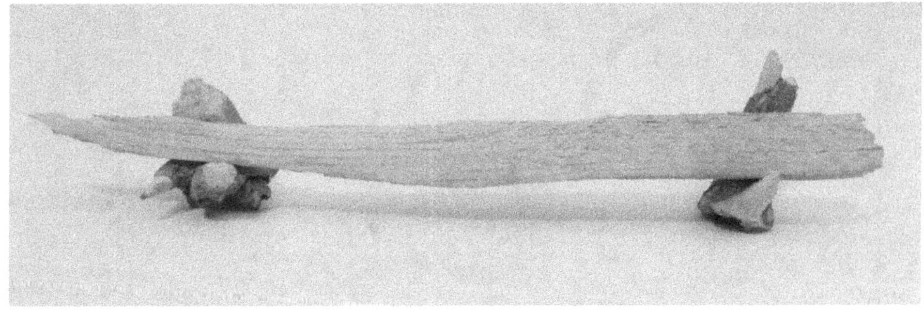

Hand-curvings by Matthew, 2011

"As you admire the wonderful things God has made today, remember you're one of them, wonderful inside and out. You are blessed, you are special, you are loved." –Author Unknown

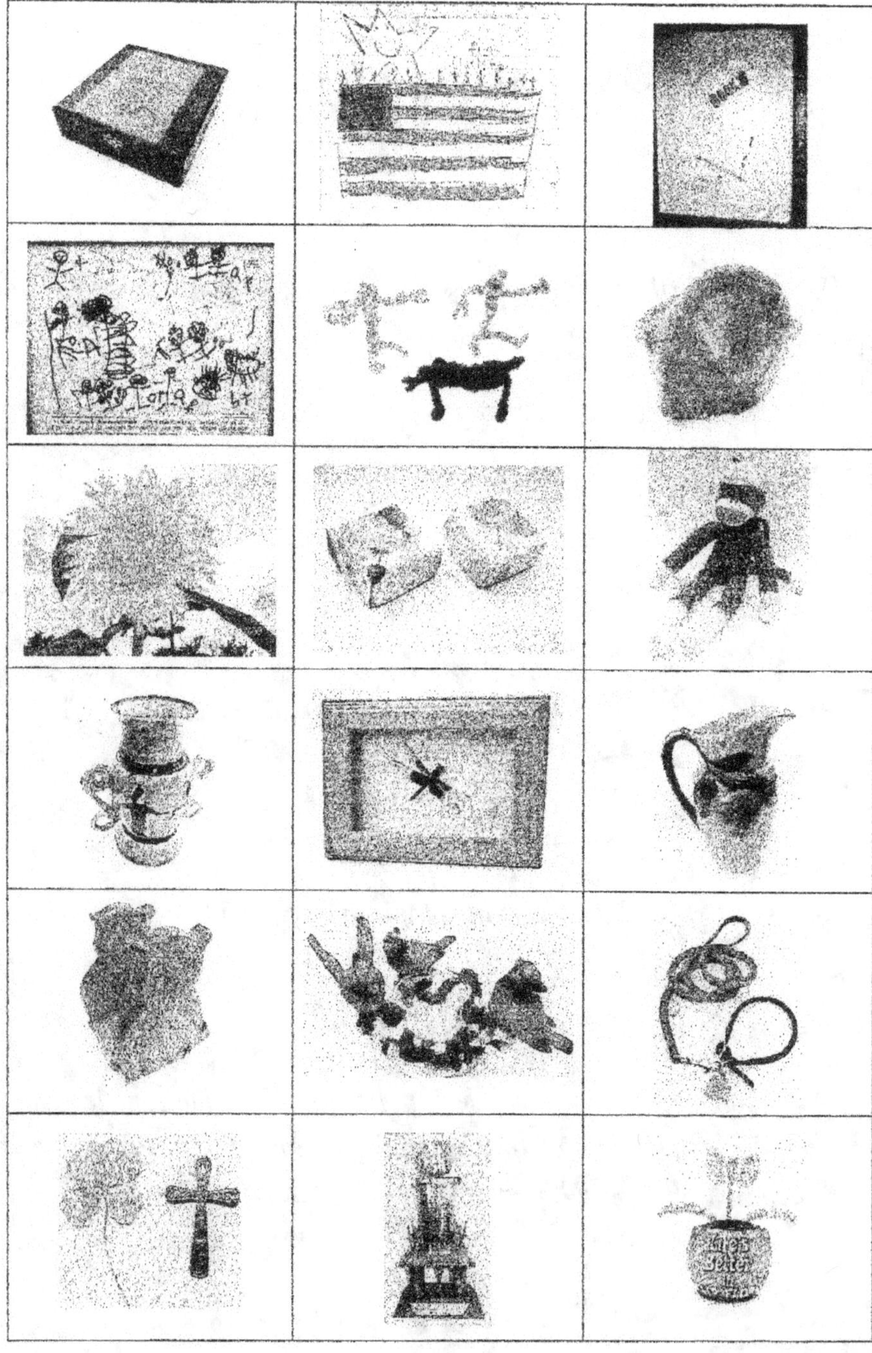

"**Risk** more than others think is safe. **Care** more than others think is wise. **Dream** more than others think is practical. **Expect** more than others think is possible." –Claude Bissell (1916-2000)

"It's not about time, it's about choices. How are you spending your choices?" –Beverly Adamo

"He who hunts for flowers will find flowers; and he who loves weeds will find weeds." – Henry Ward Beecher (1813-1887)

"Never despair, but if you do, work on in despair."
Edmund Burke (1729 – 1797)

"Fear knocked at the door. Faith answered.
And lo, no one was there."
--Anonymous